THIS COLORING BOOK BELONGS TO

IMPURVING ART

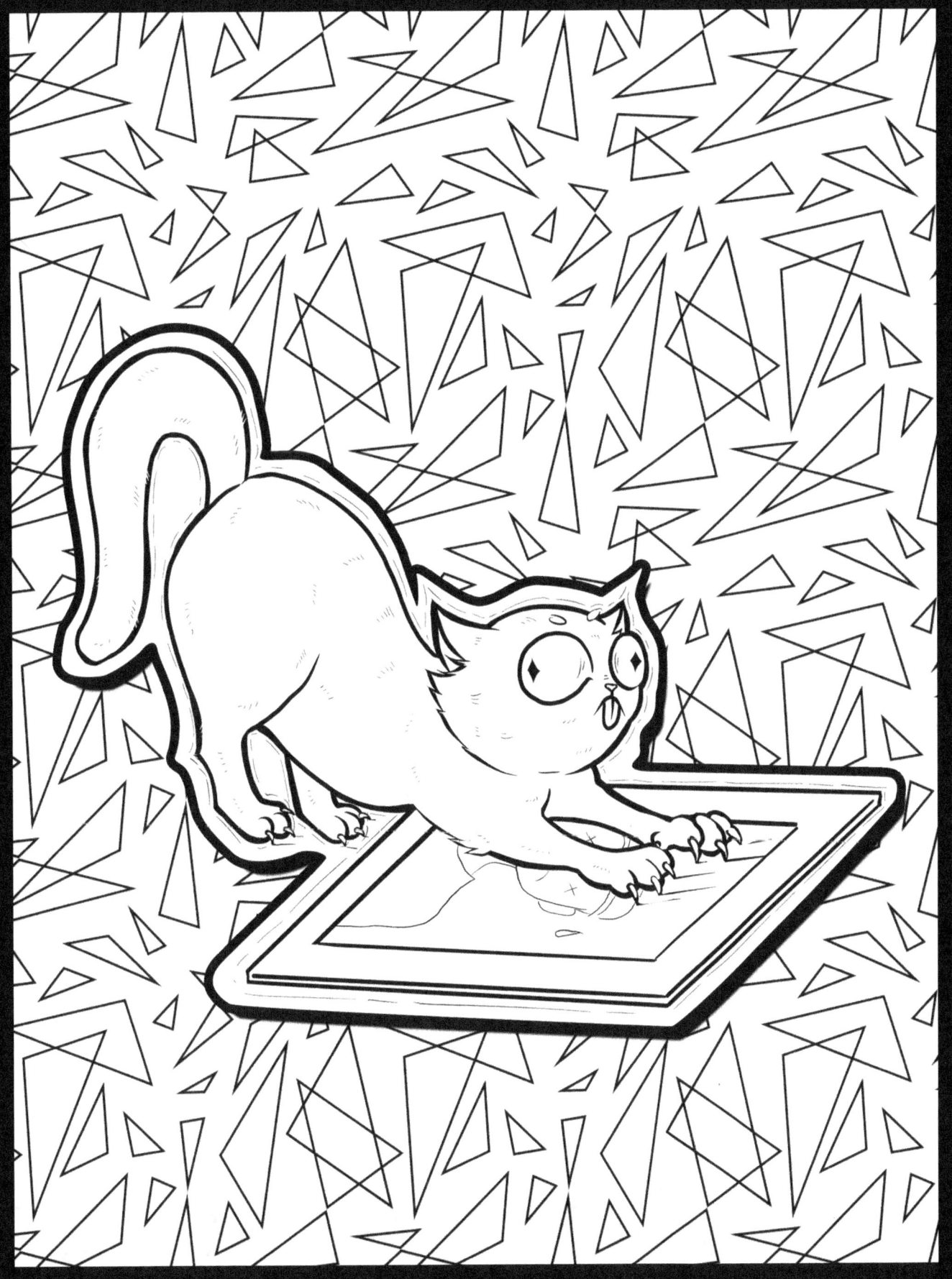

PRESENT FUR MY HUMAN

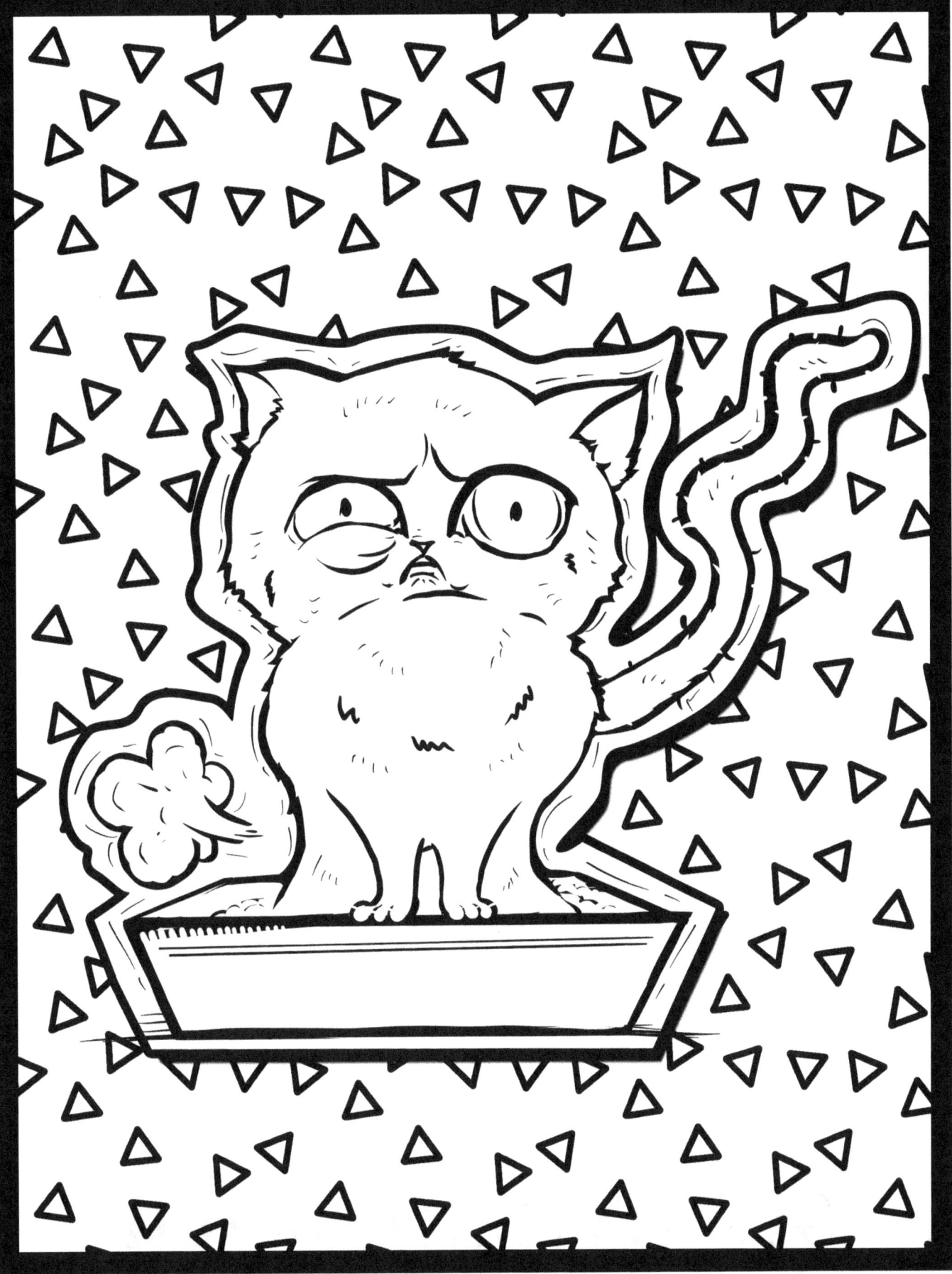

SCRATCH...SCRATCH

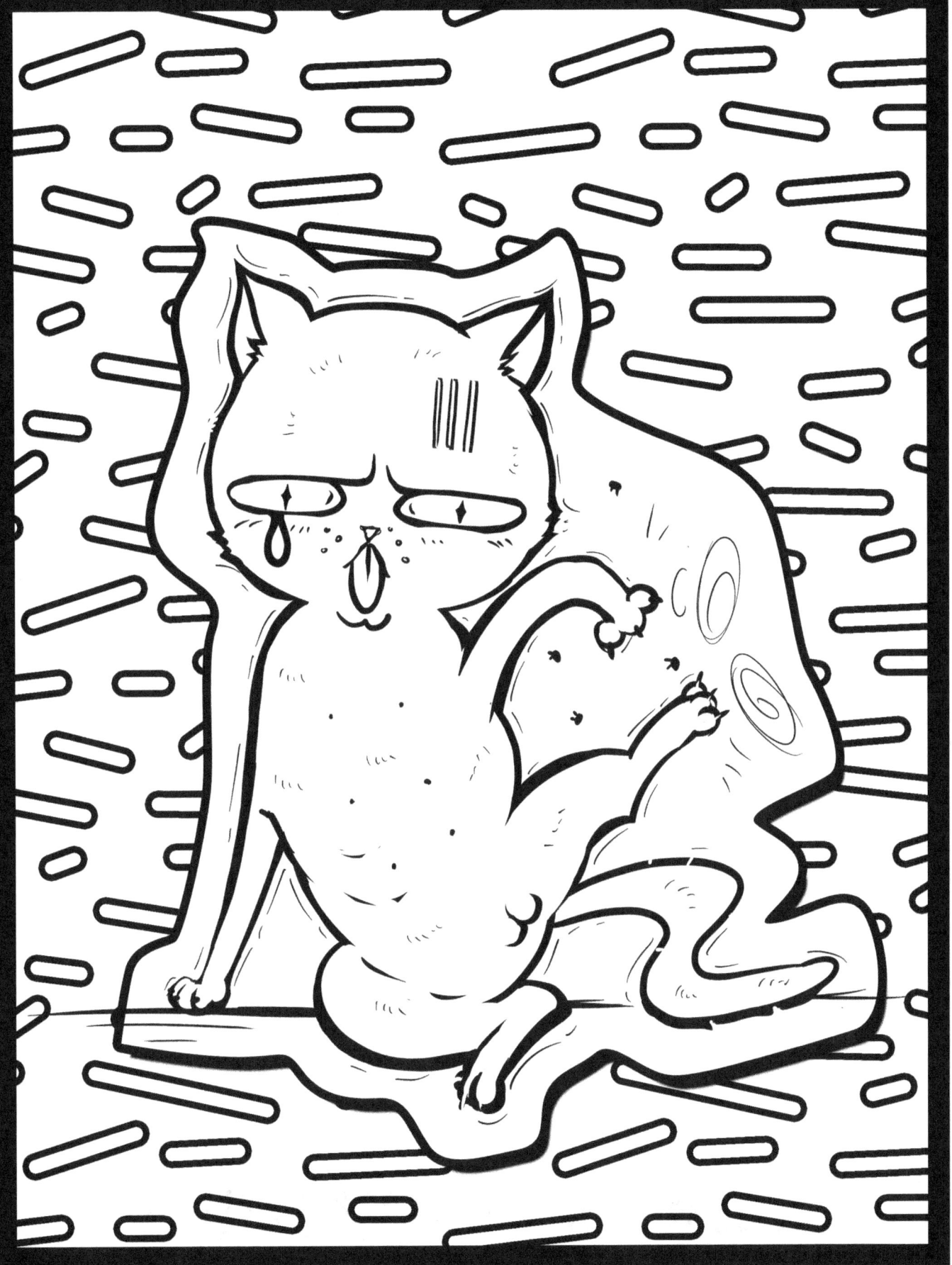

WHAT A MEOWMENT

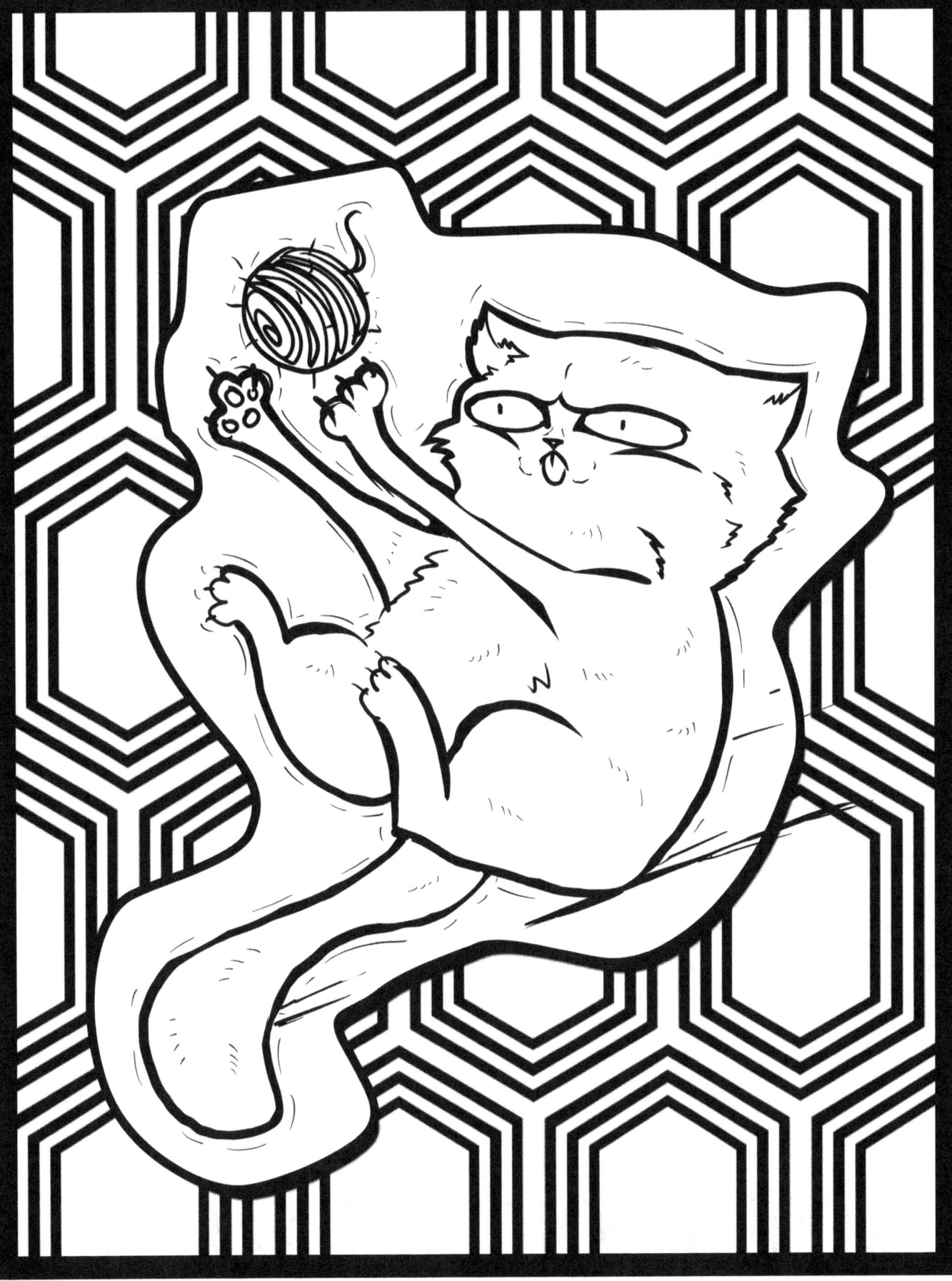

I'VE DONE THAT BEFUR

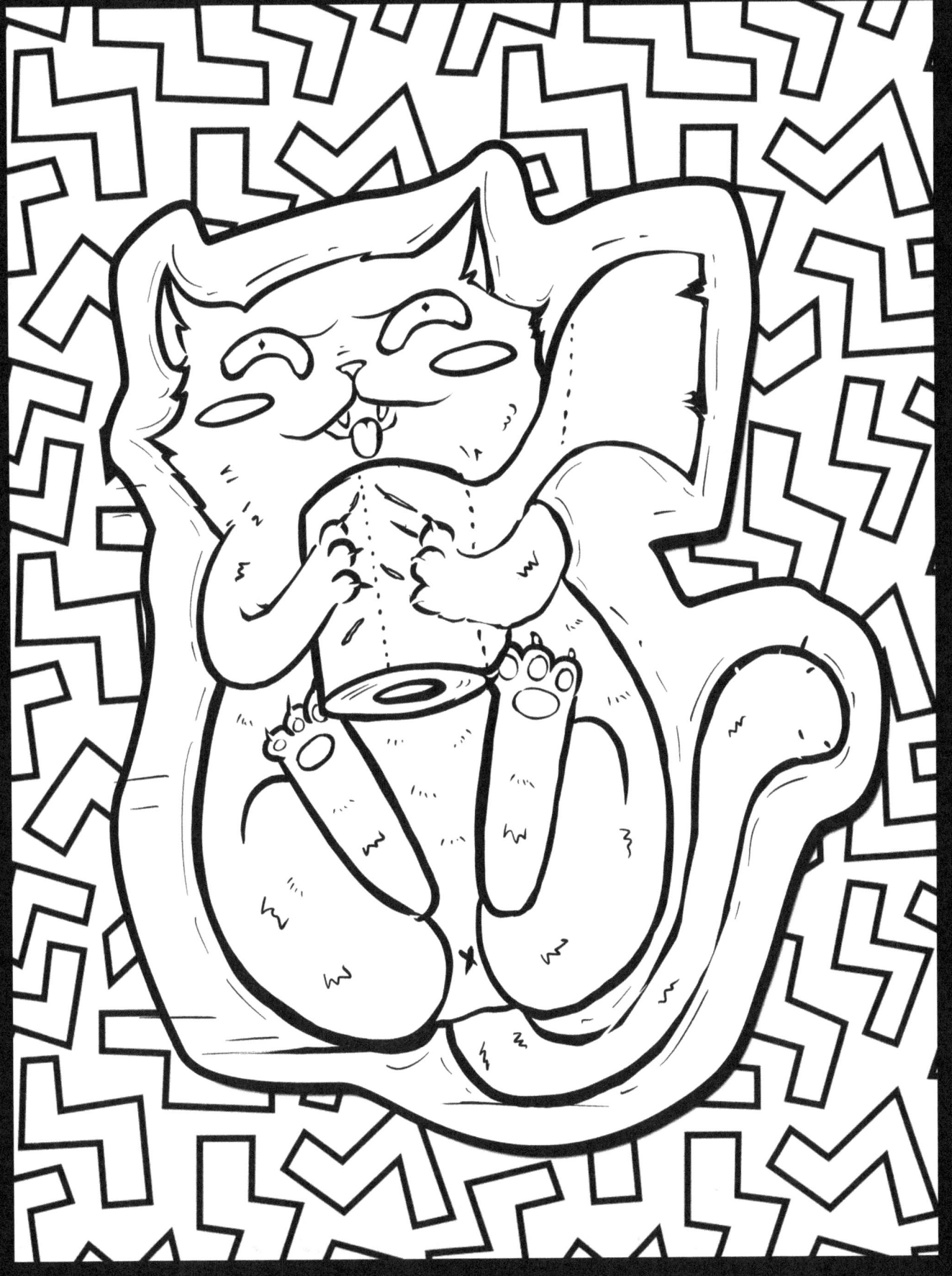

DO CATS FLY?

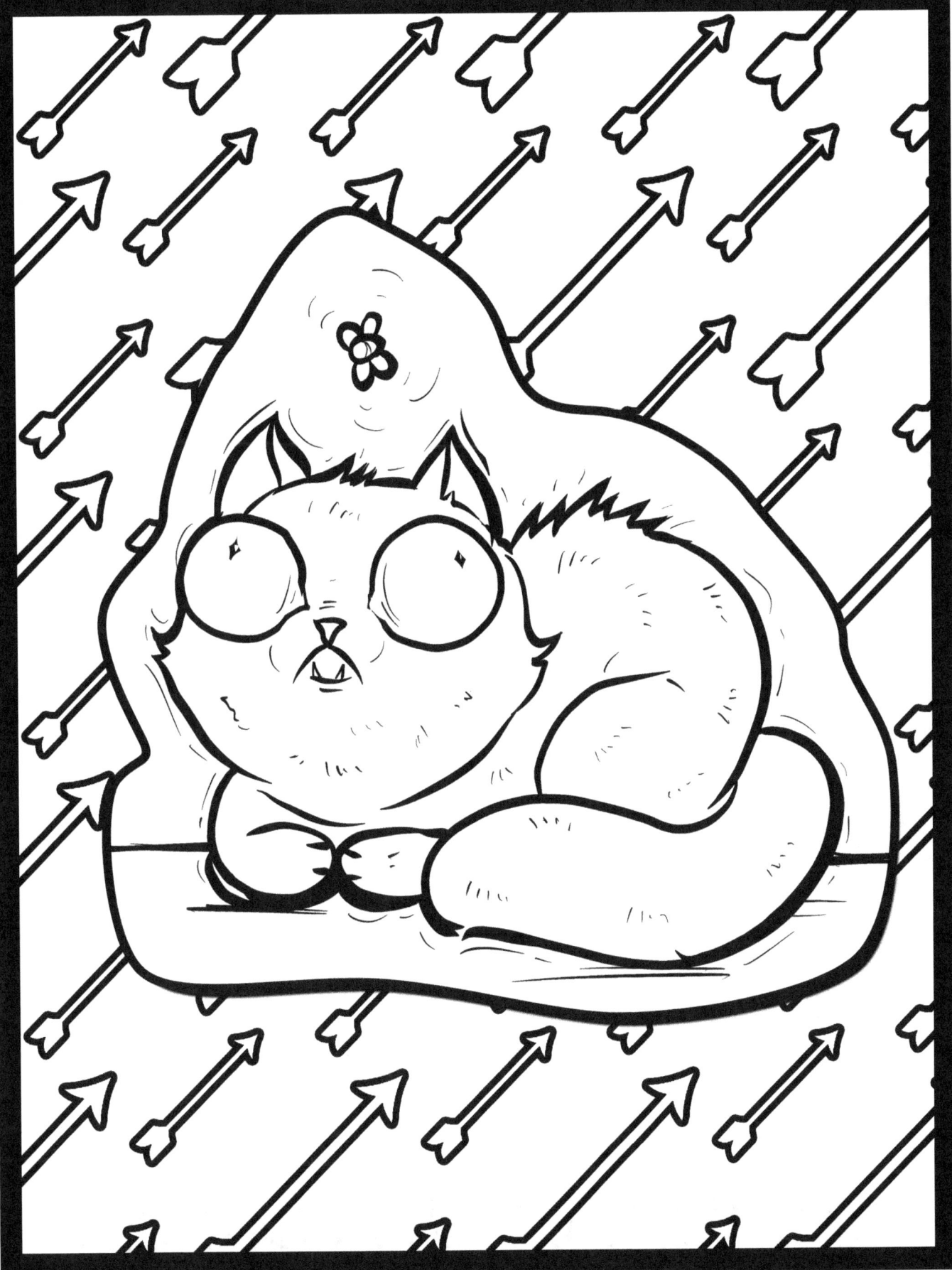

WHAT A CATASTROPHE

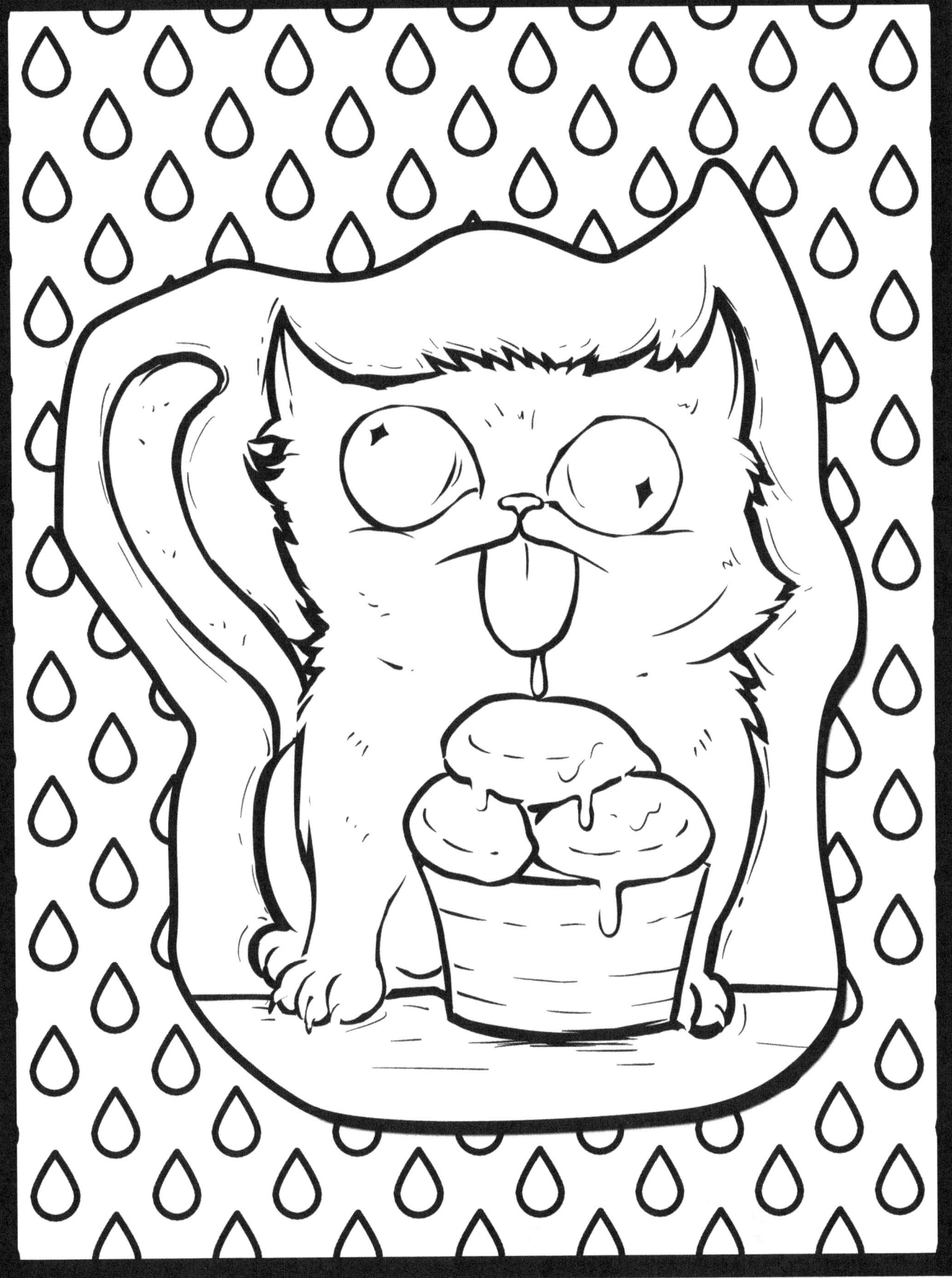

REDEFURRATION

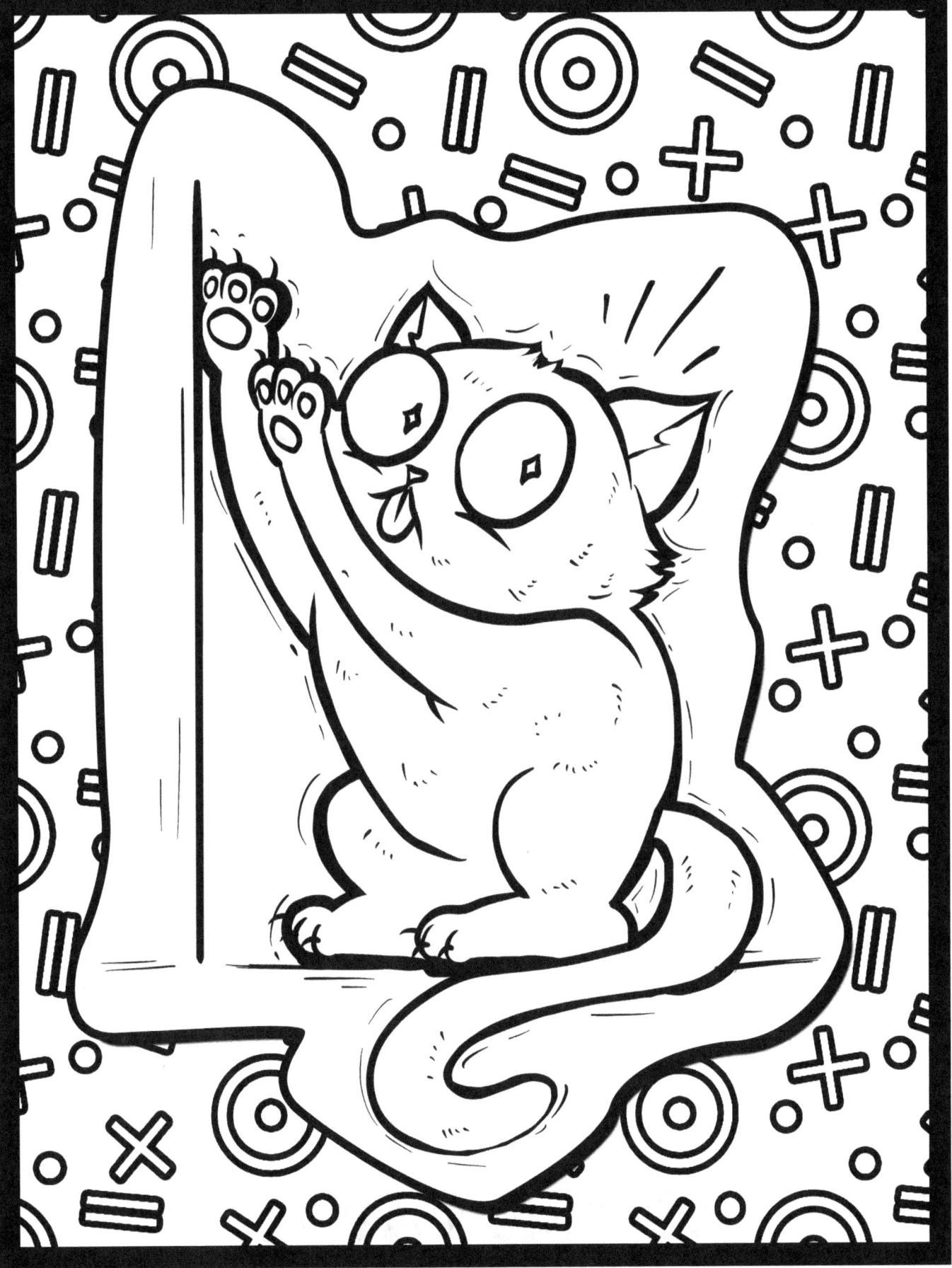

SUPER PAWER

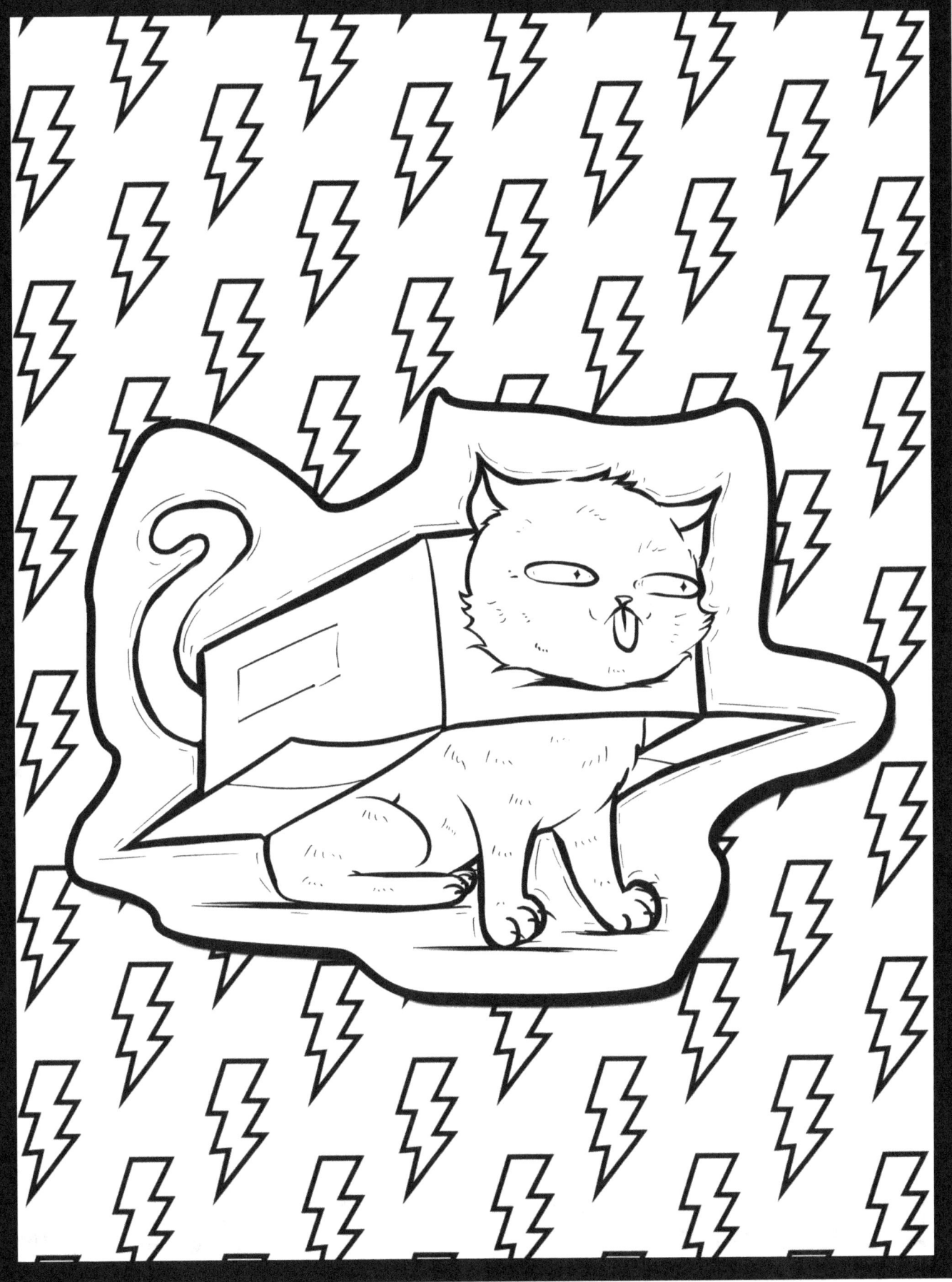

I'M JUST KITTEN AROUND

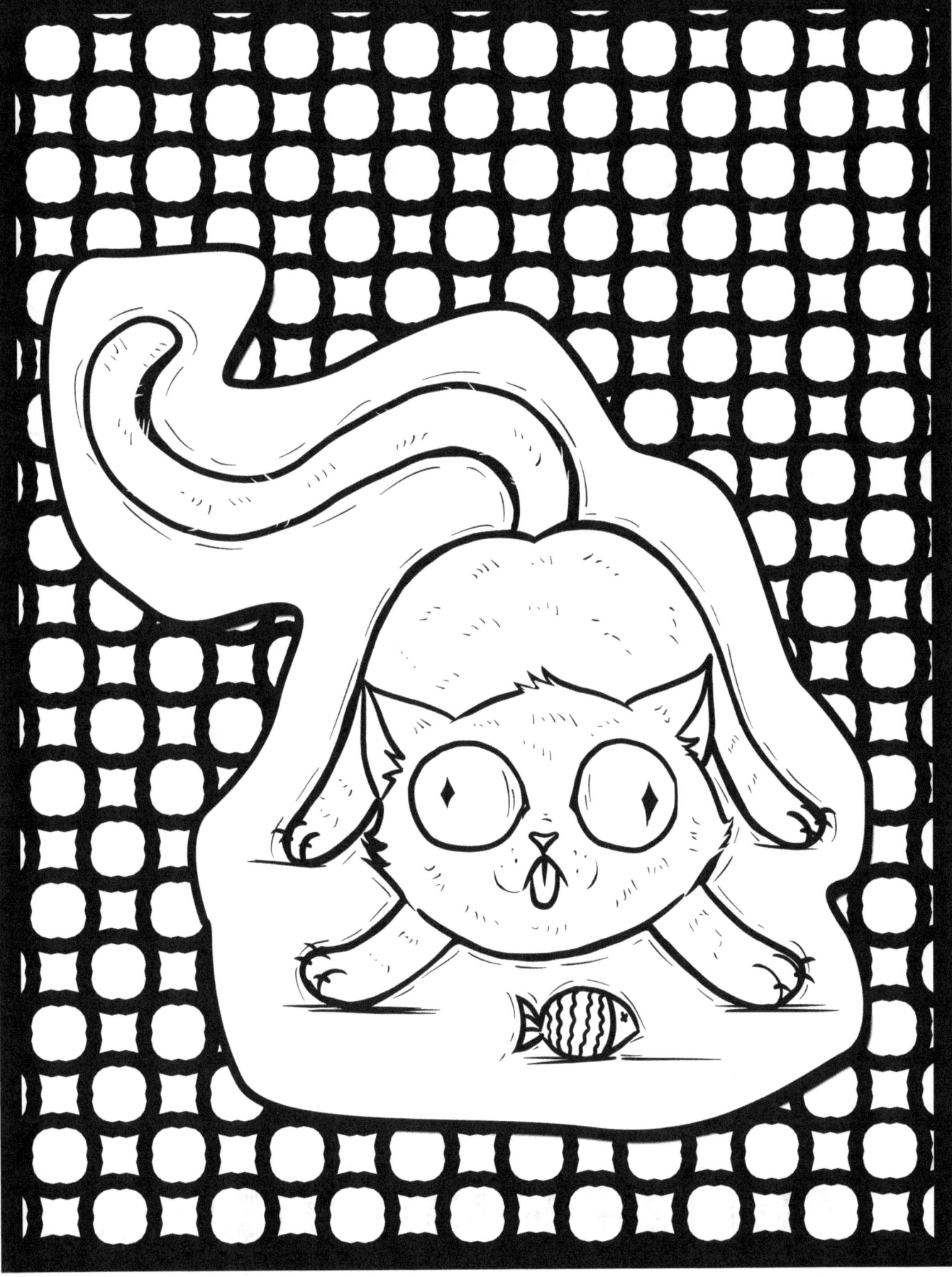

YOU LOOK FURMILIAR

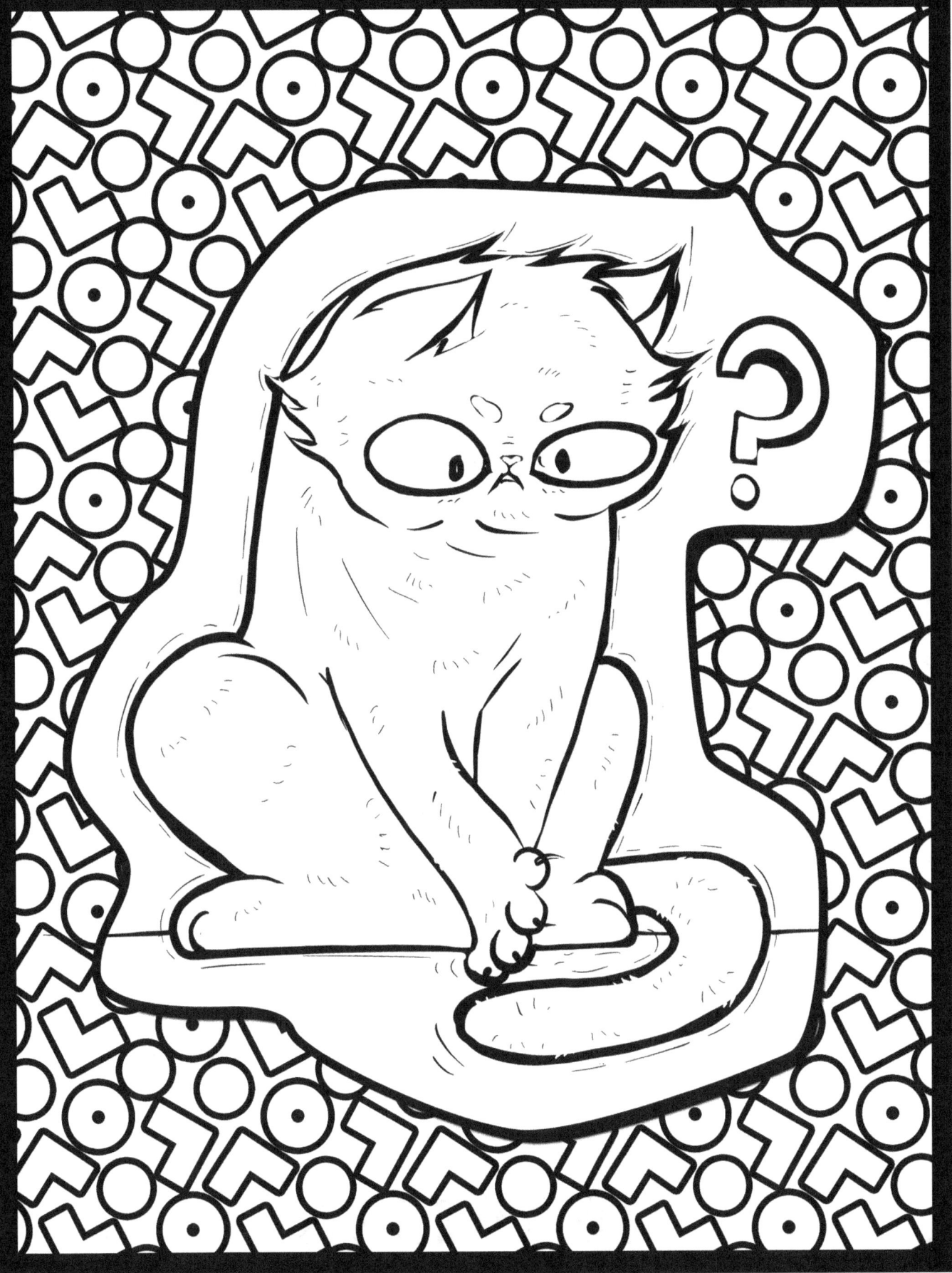

APAWLING

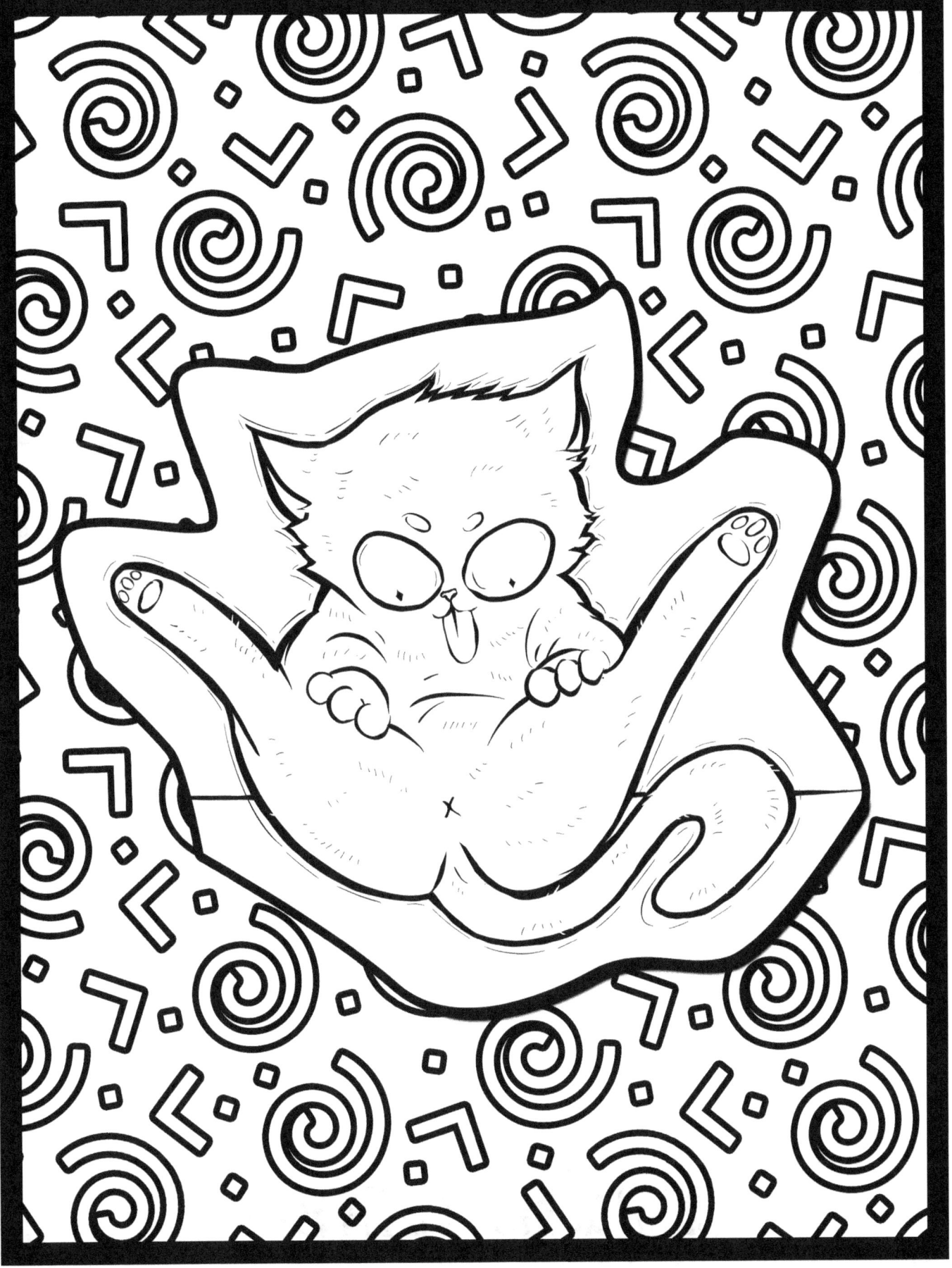

PURRPLEXED

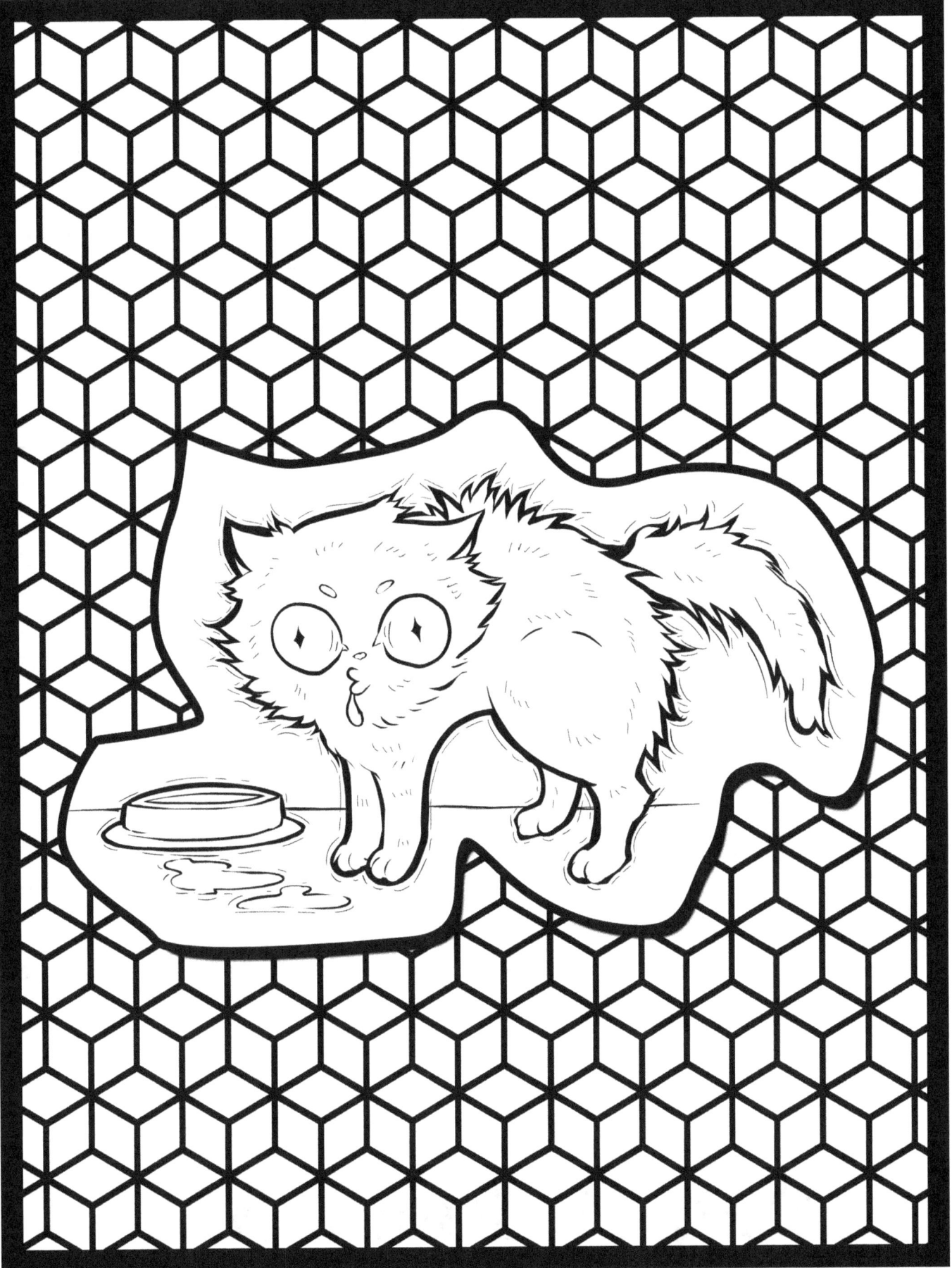

THE LAST PAWSAGE

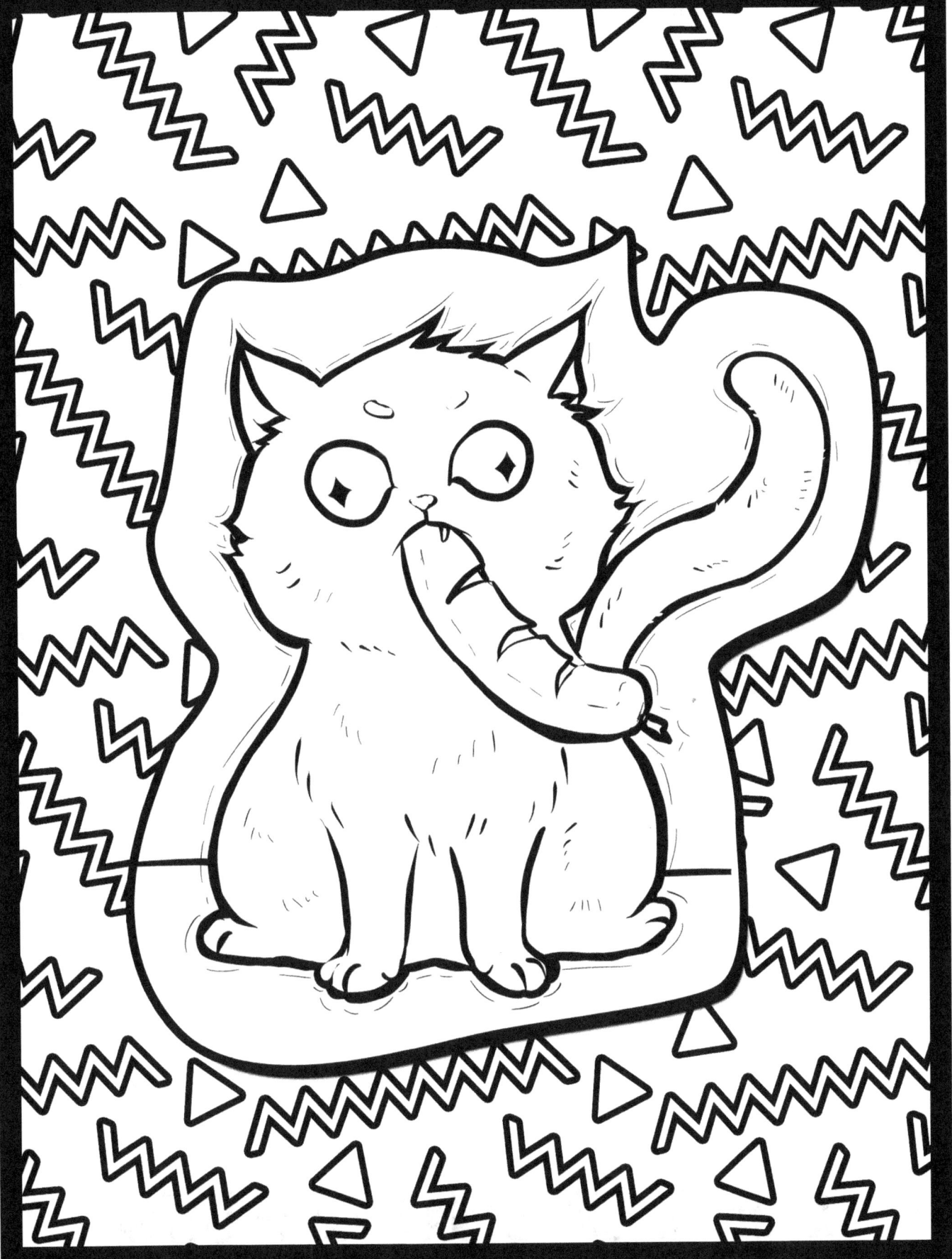

I'M A GLAMOURPUSS

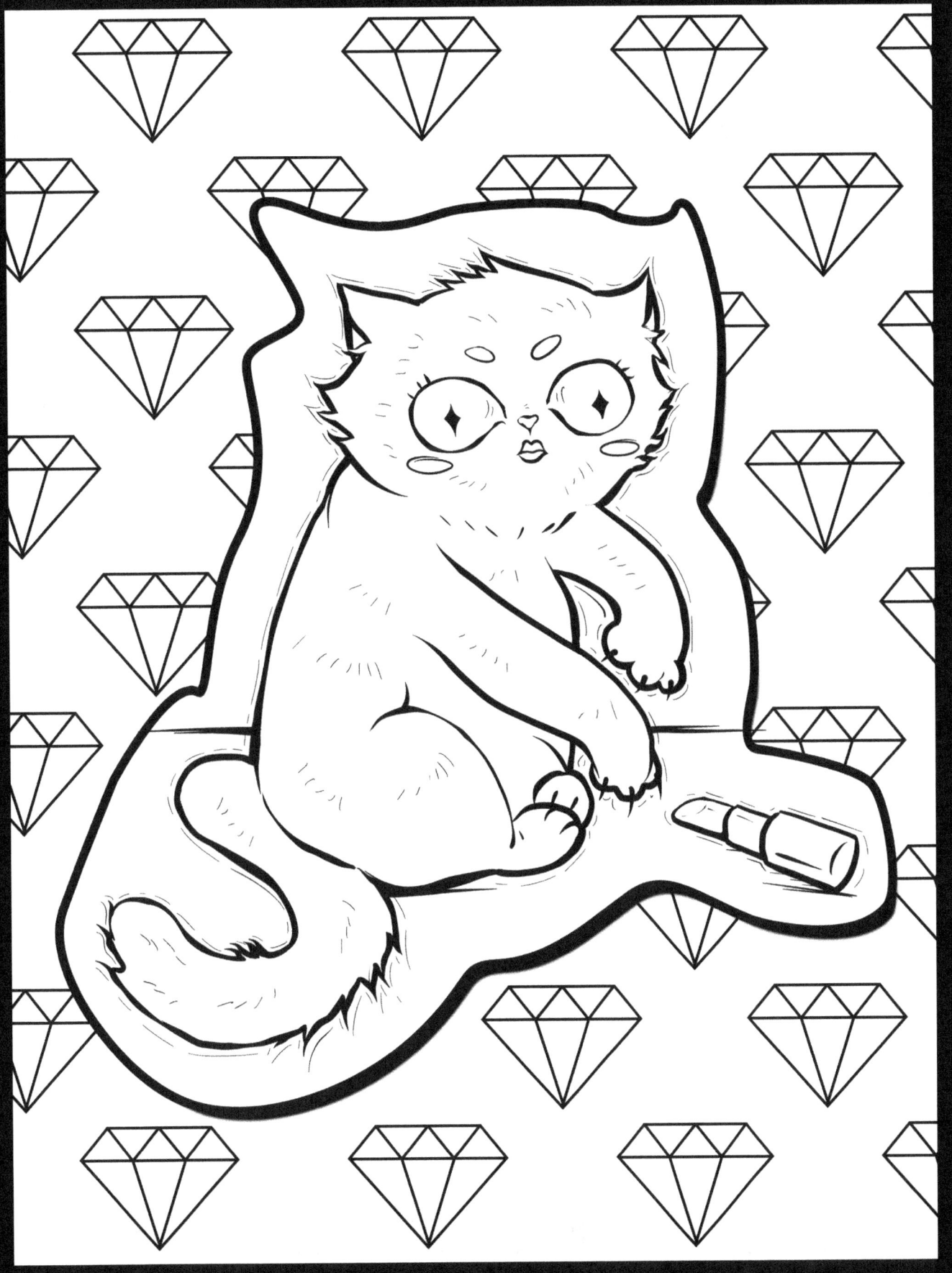

IT'S MEOW OR NEVER

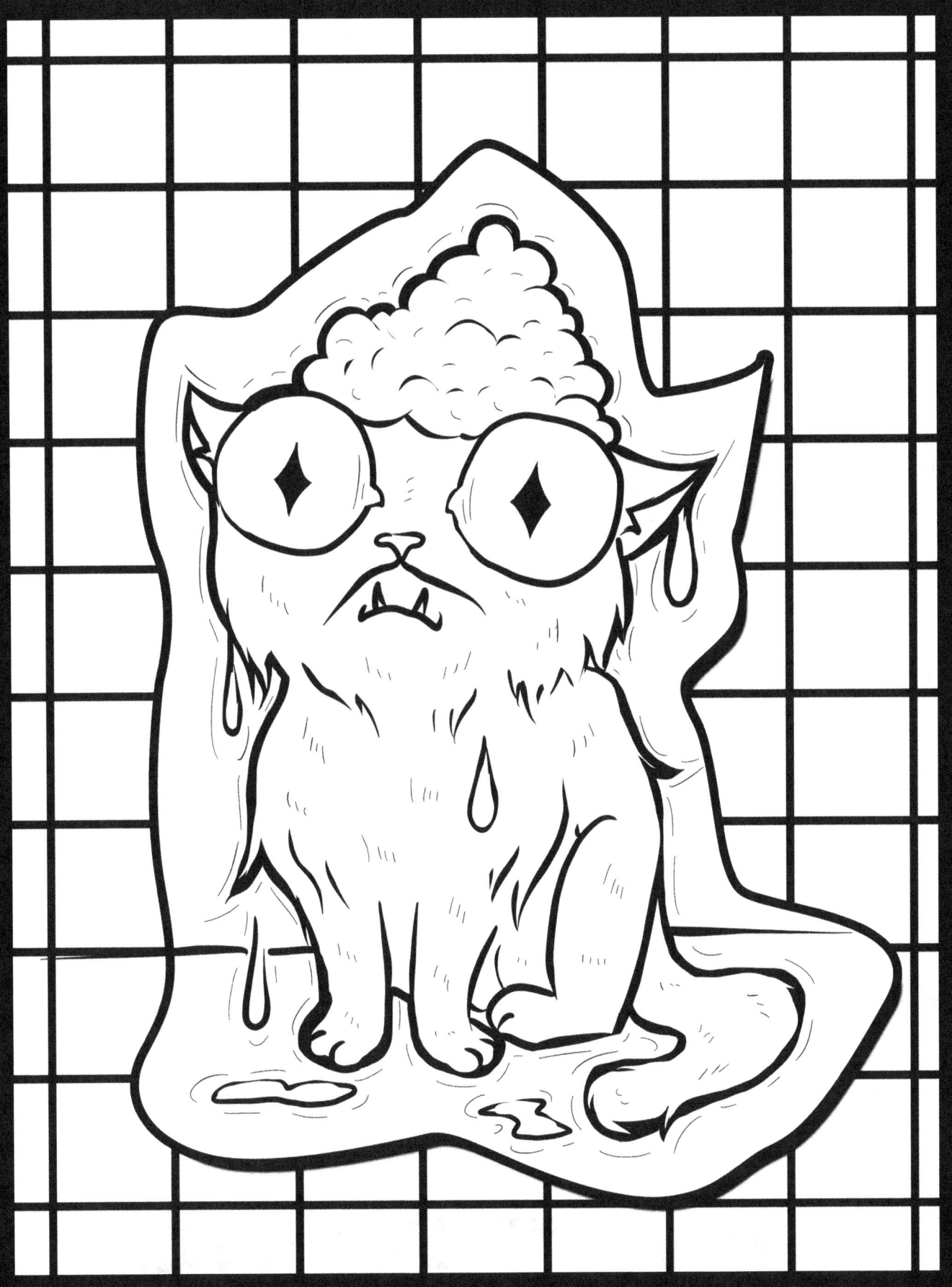

I LOVE MY FURRARI

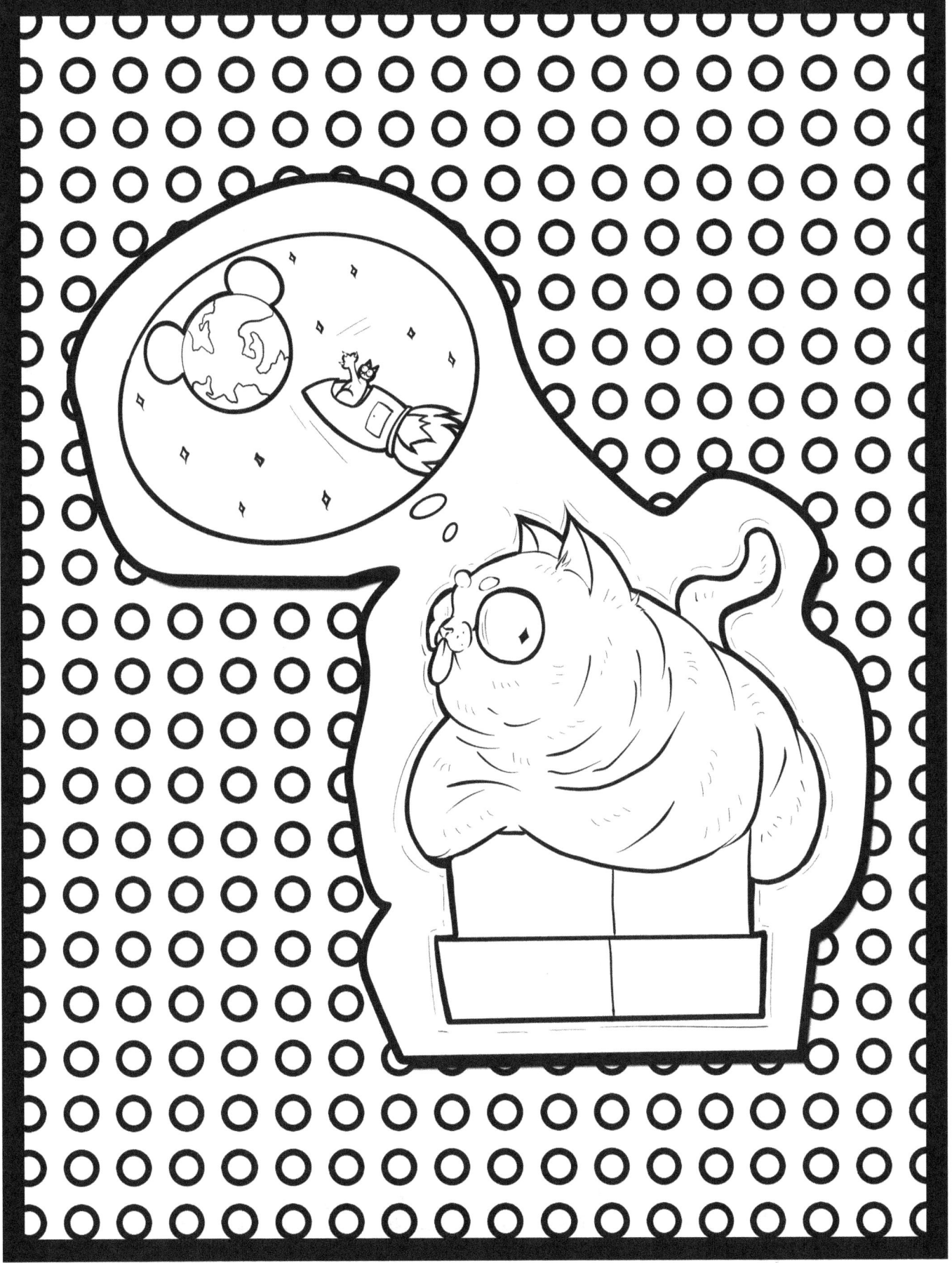

LITTLE MEWMAID

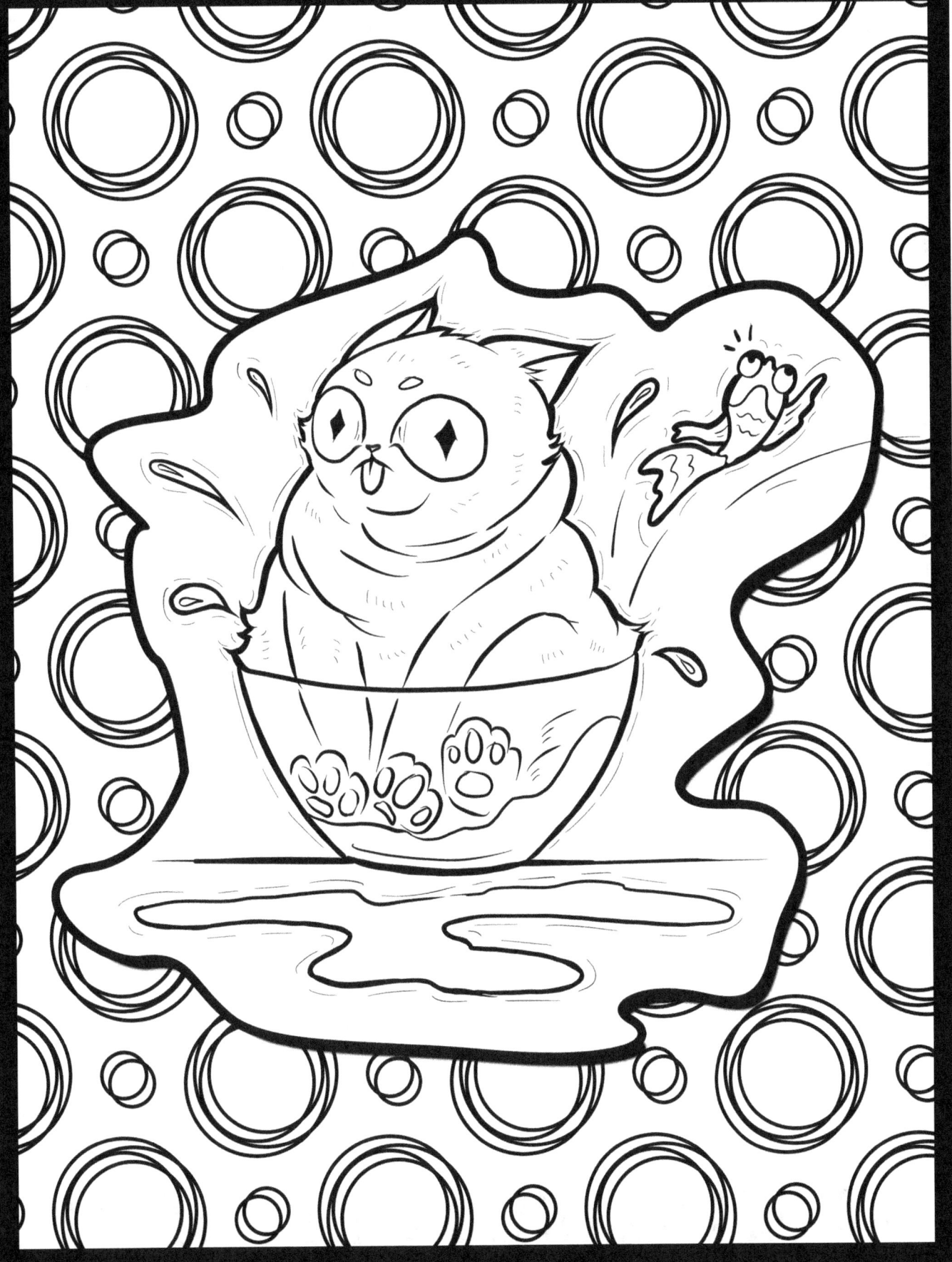

FURMIDABLE OPPONENT

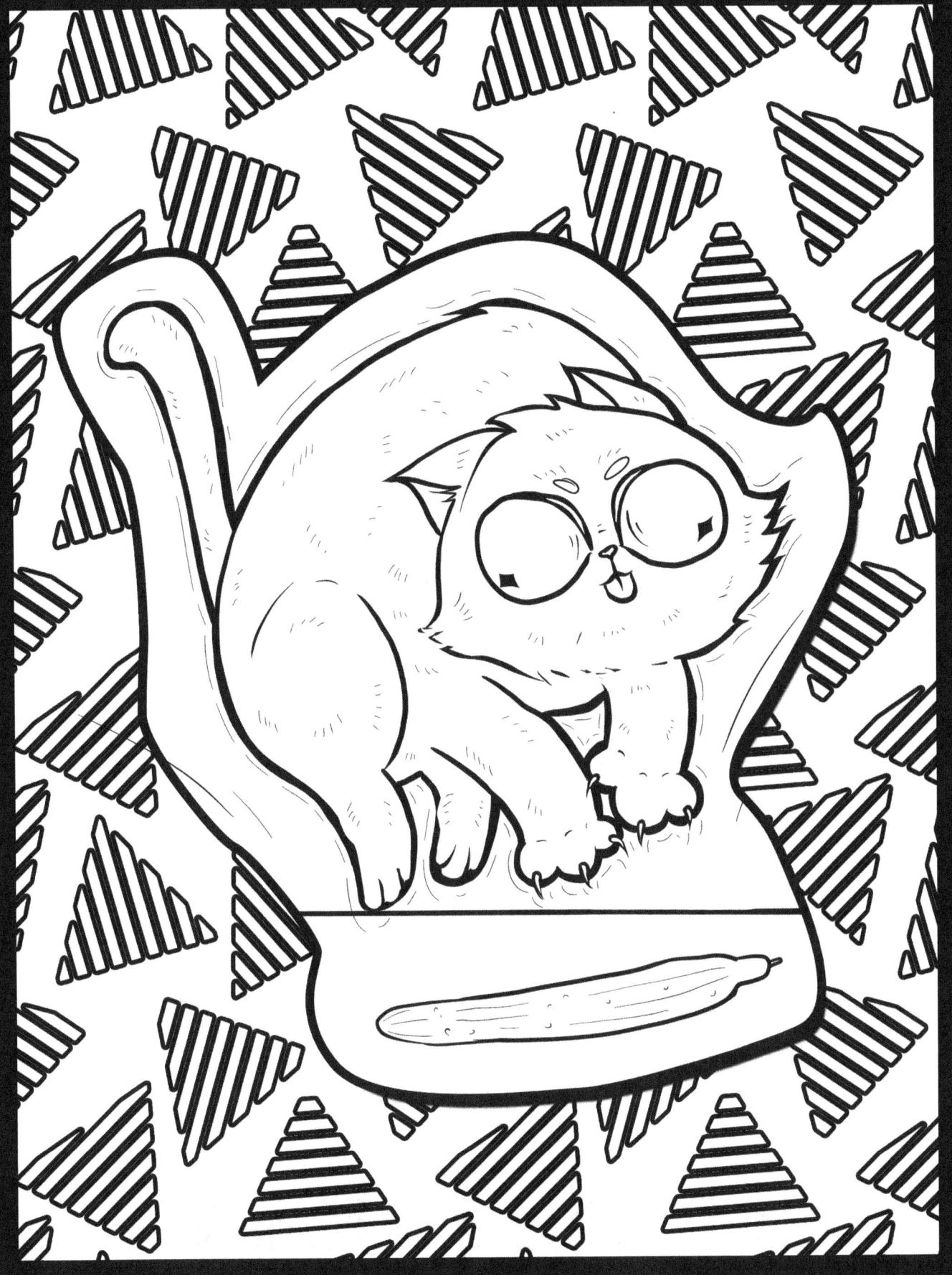

LIKE MY PAWJAMAS?

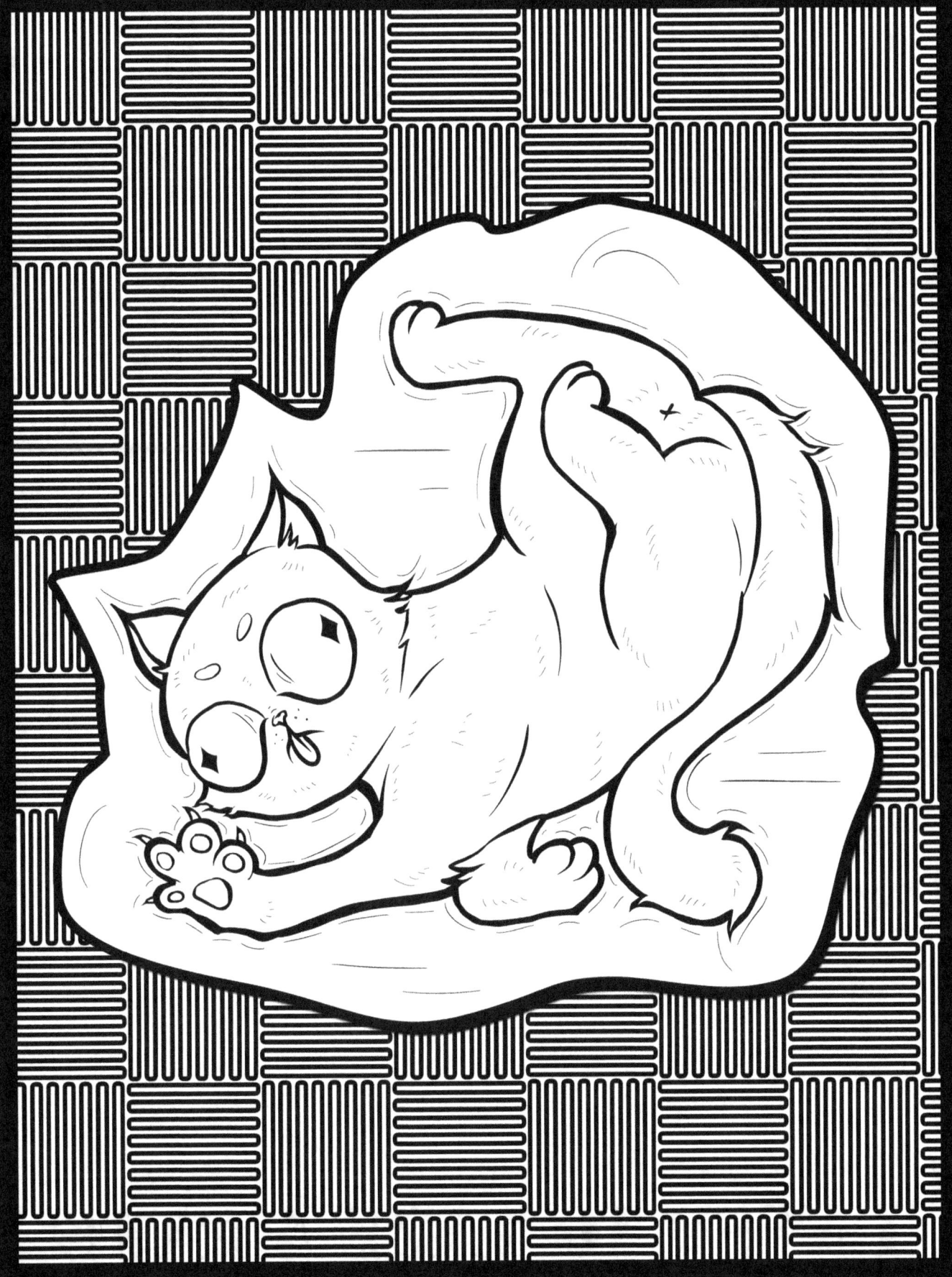

I NEED TO TAKE A PAWS

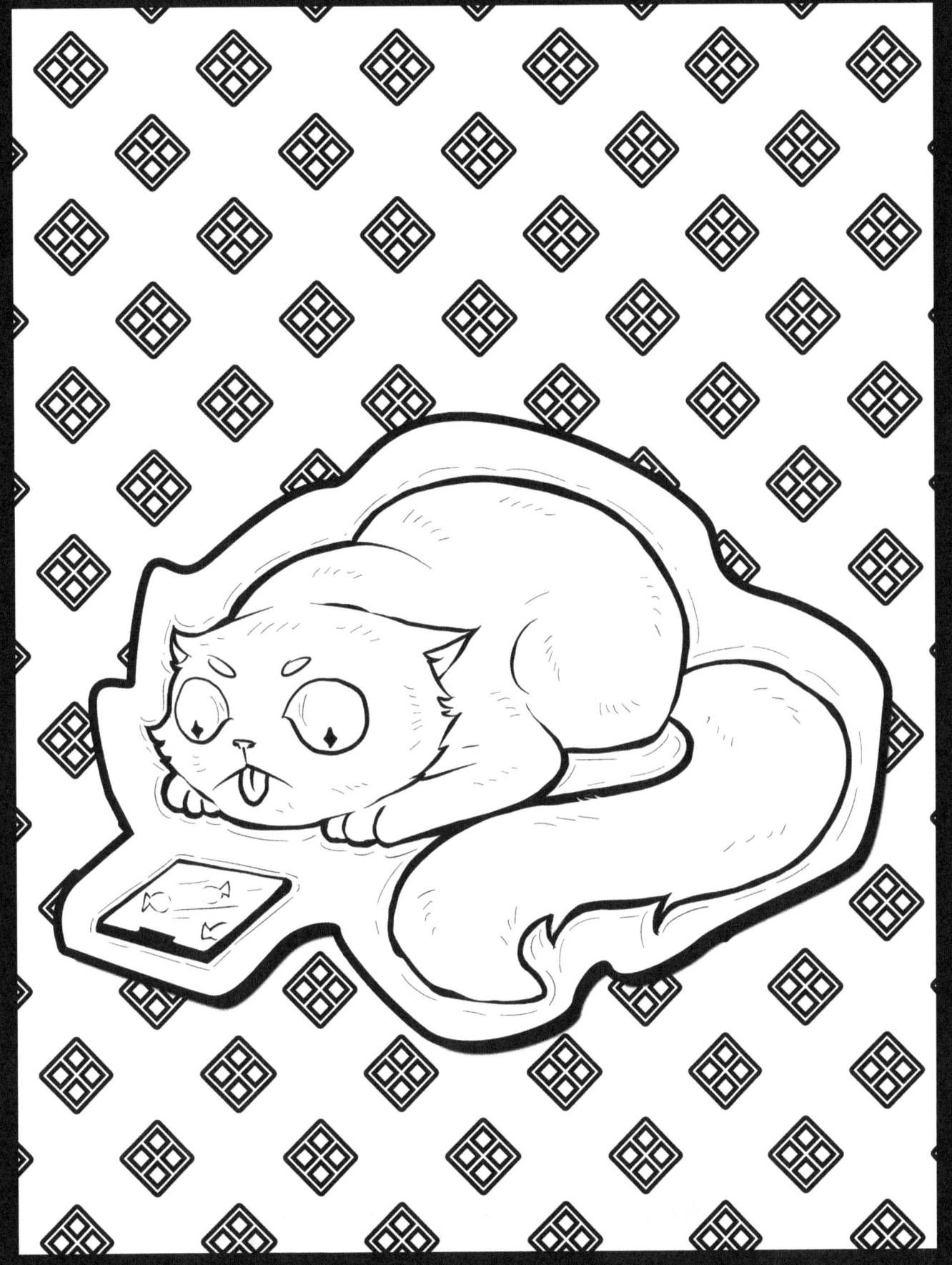

FURMIDABLE

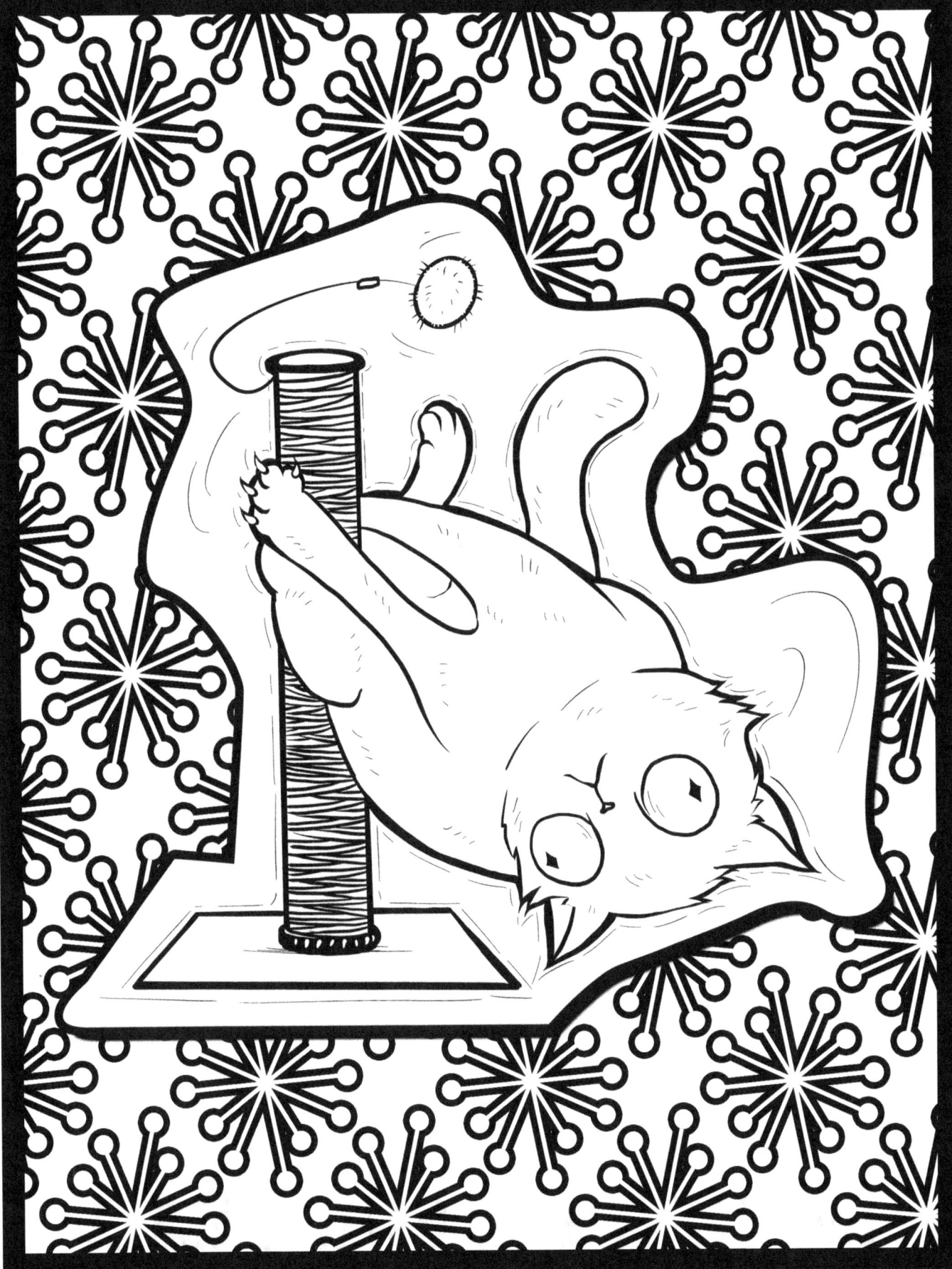

LISTEN, I'M FUR REAL!

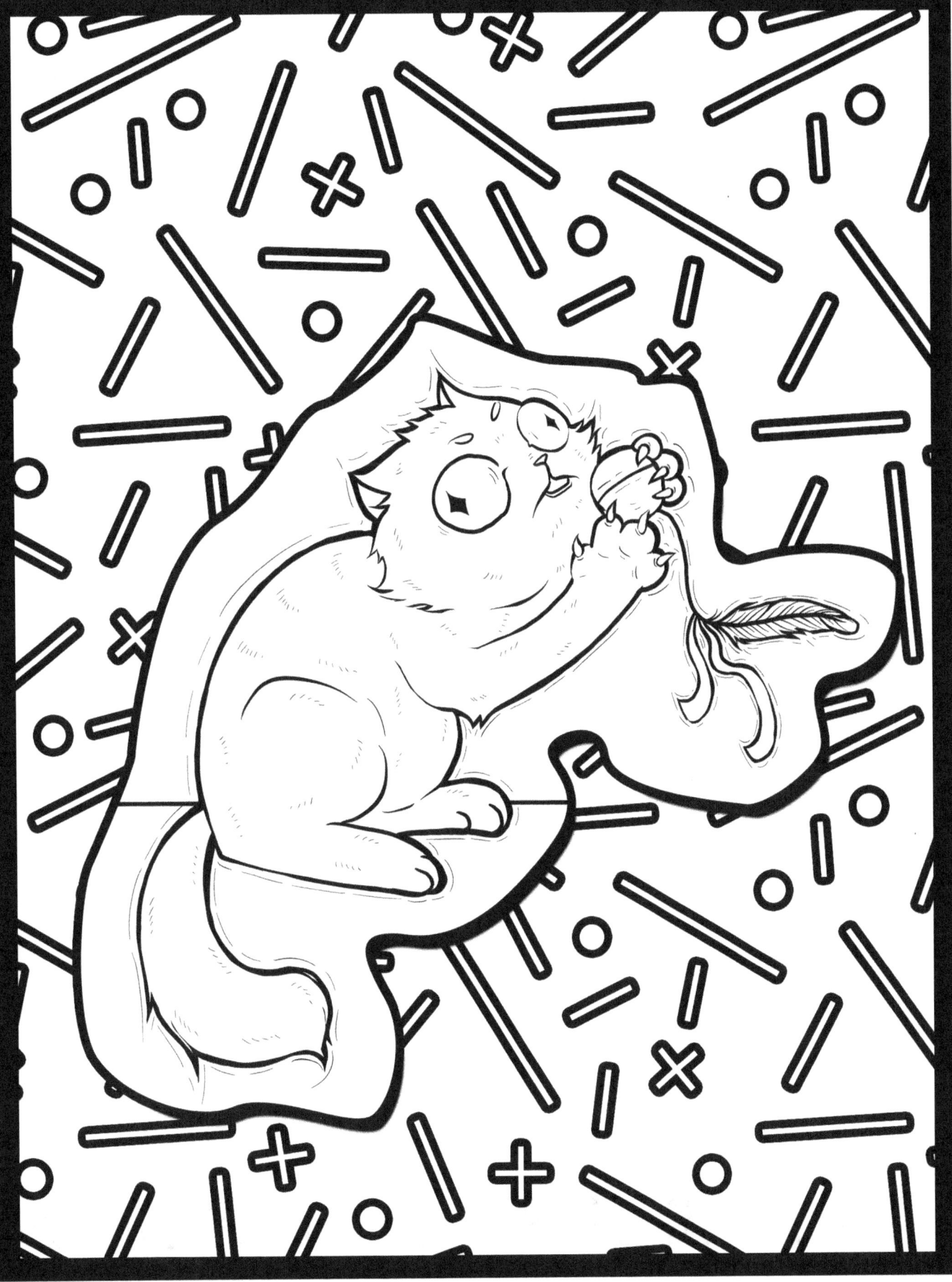

TAKE MEOWT FOR LUNCH

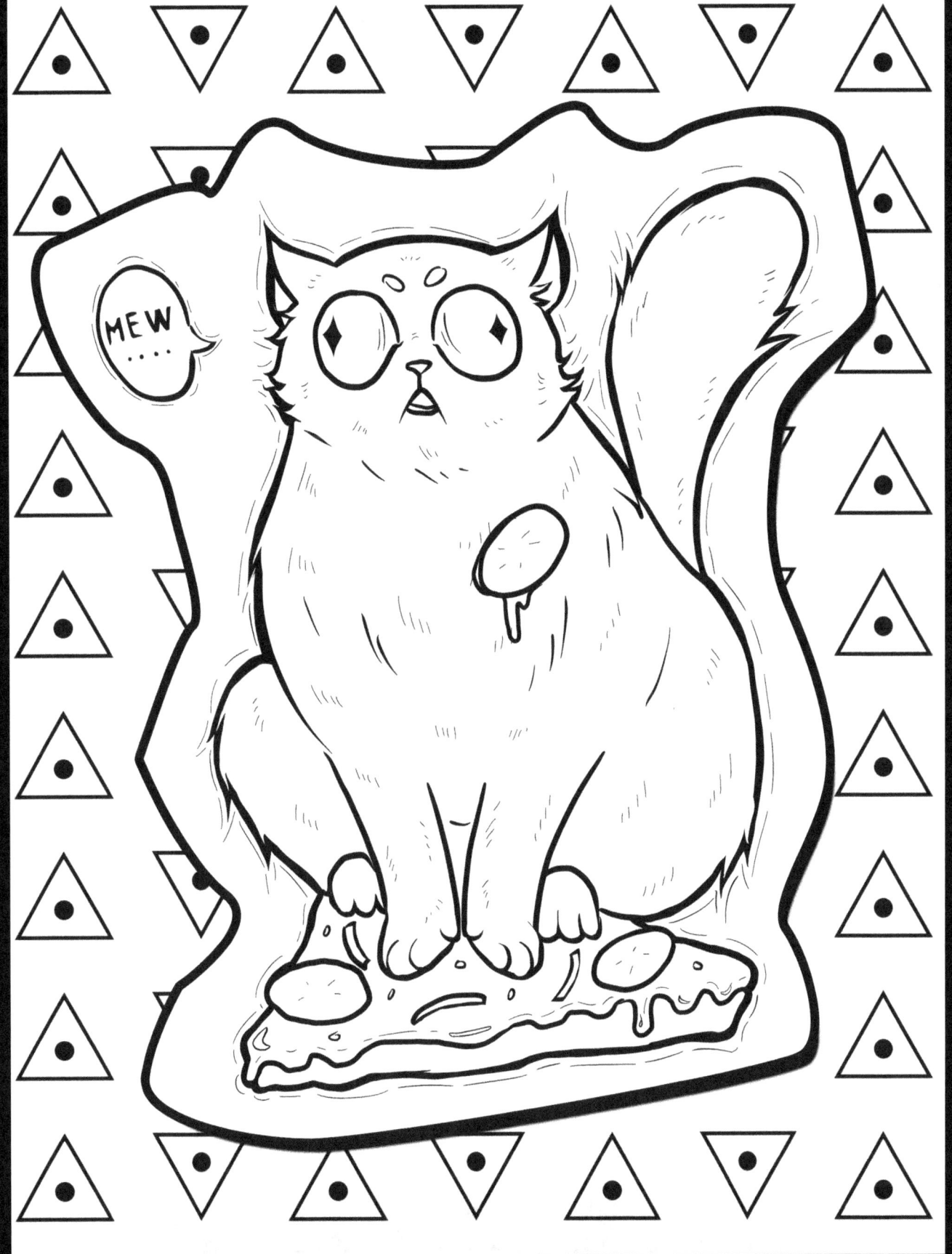

SUPER CATHLETIC

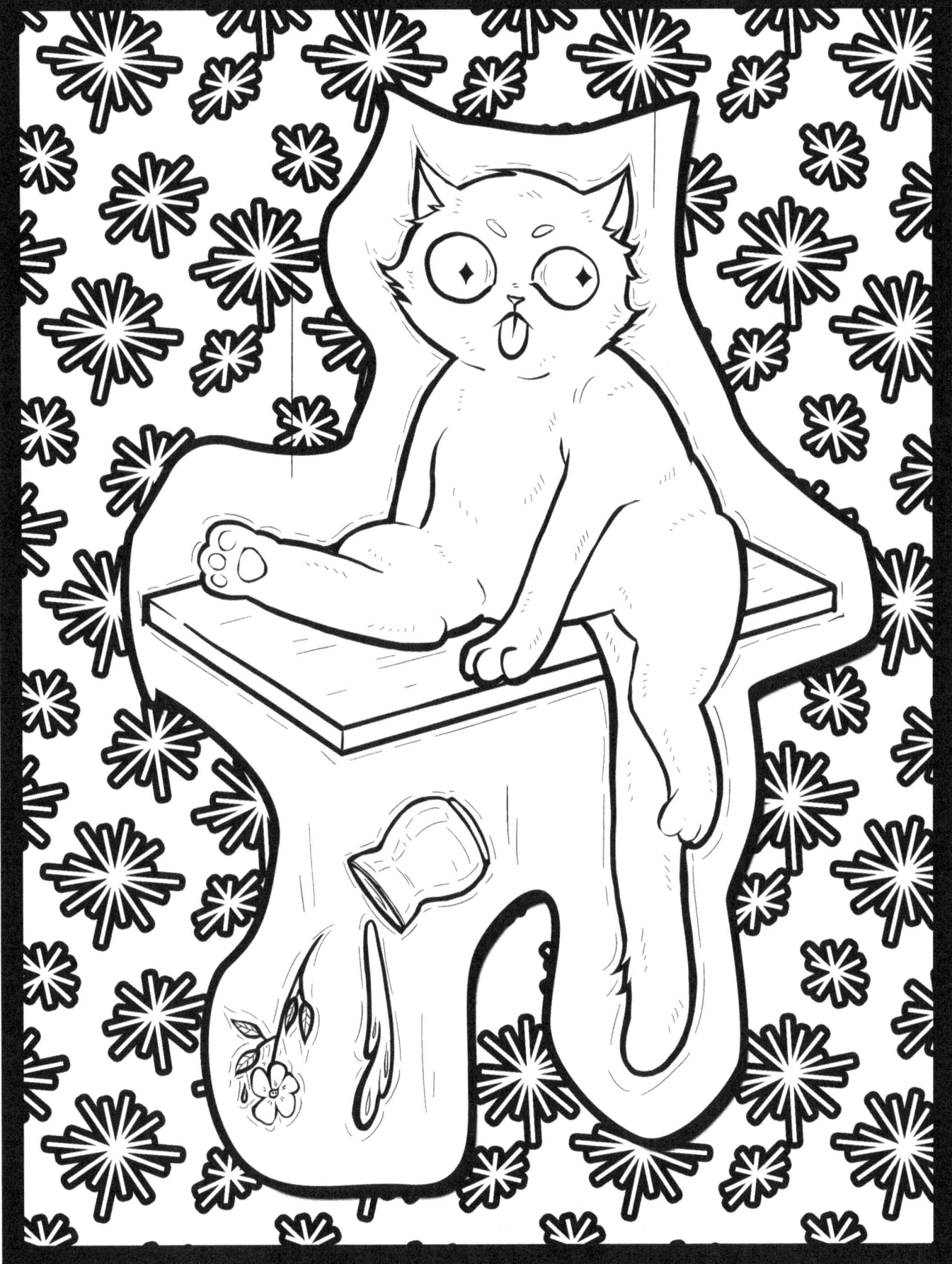

PISI...PISI

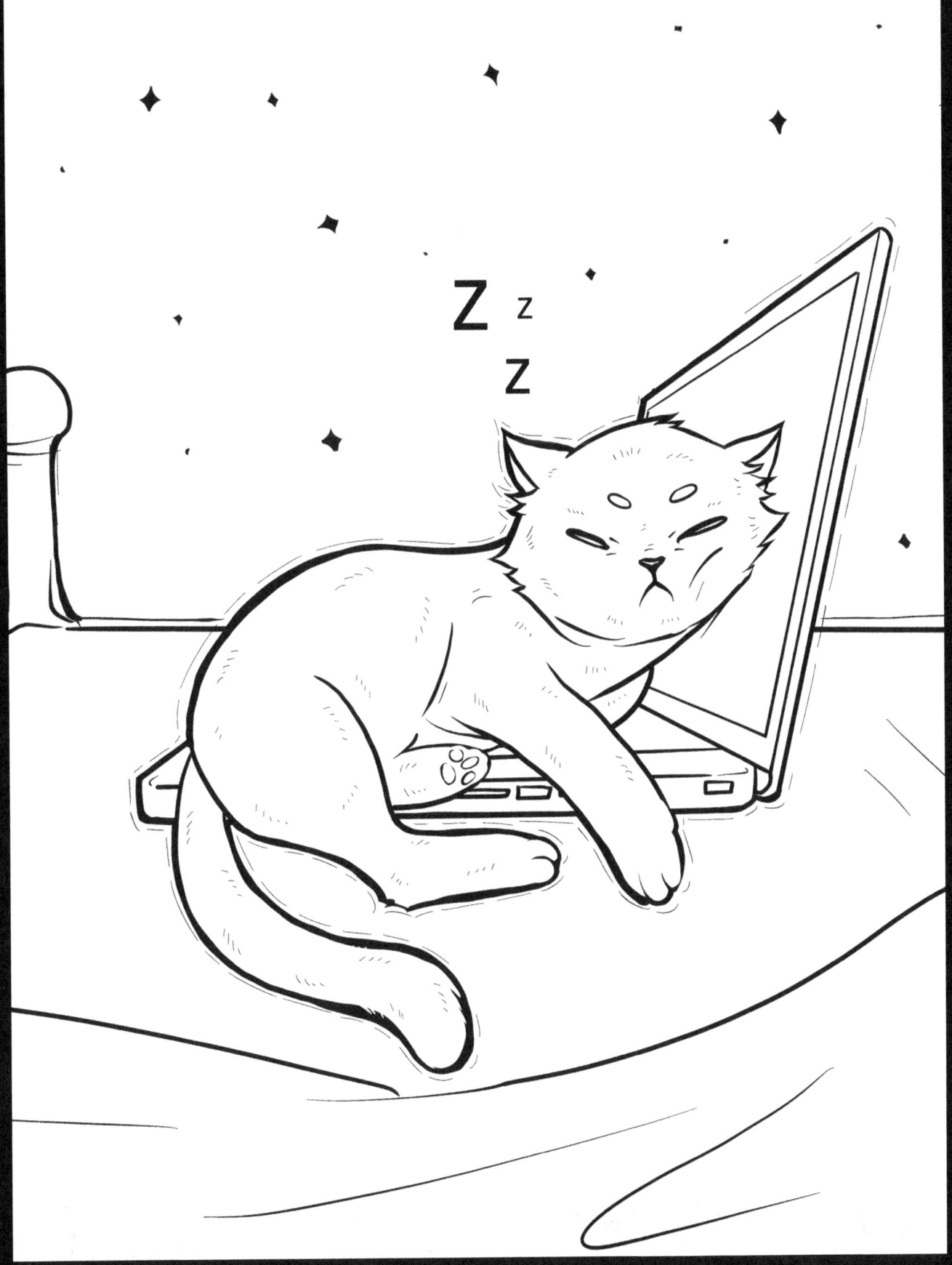

LET ME TELL YOU A TAIL

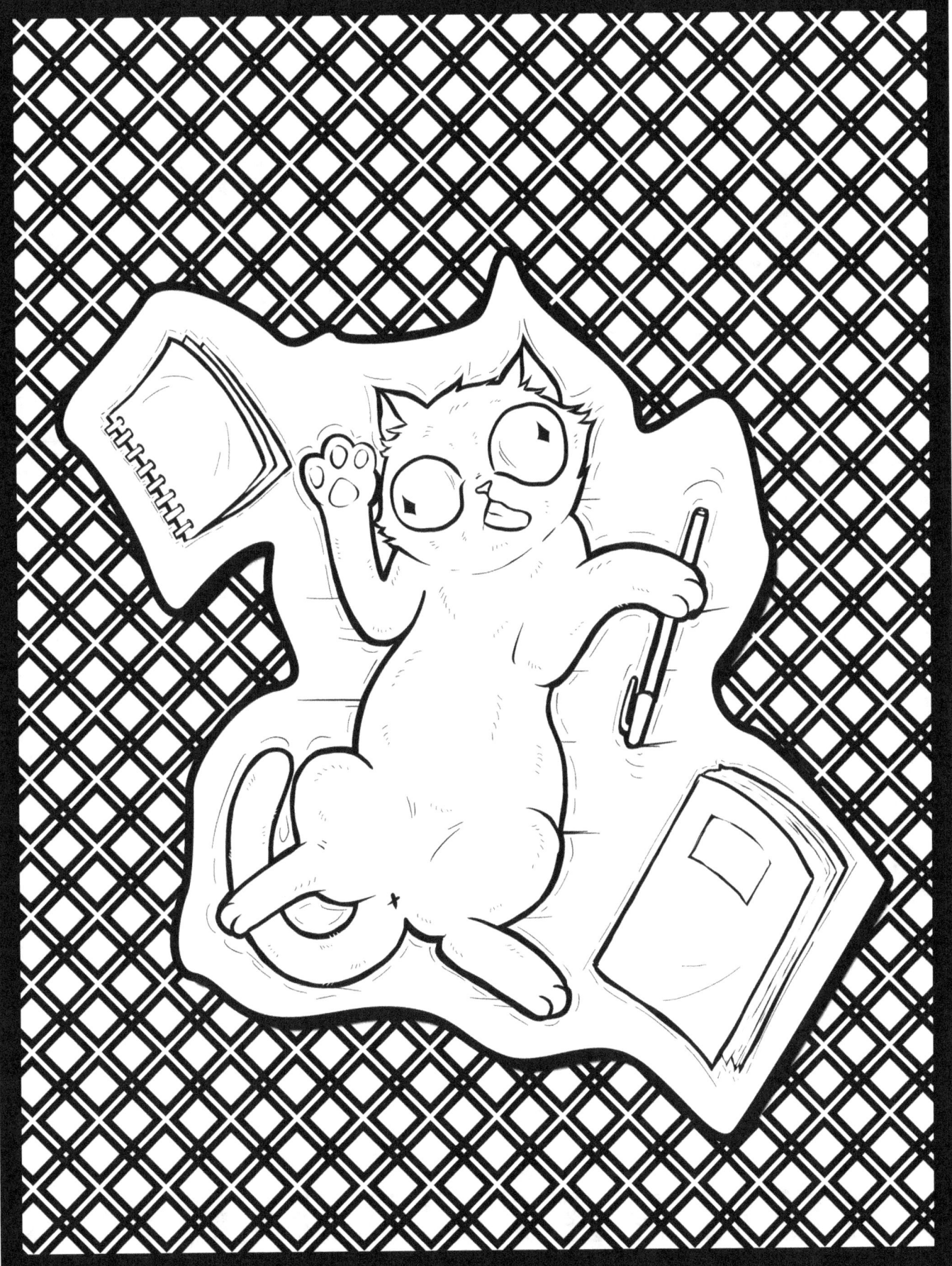

THAT'S A PAWSIBILITY

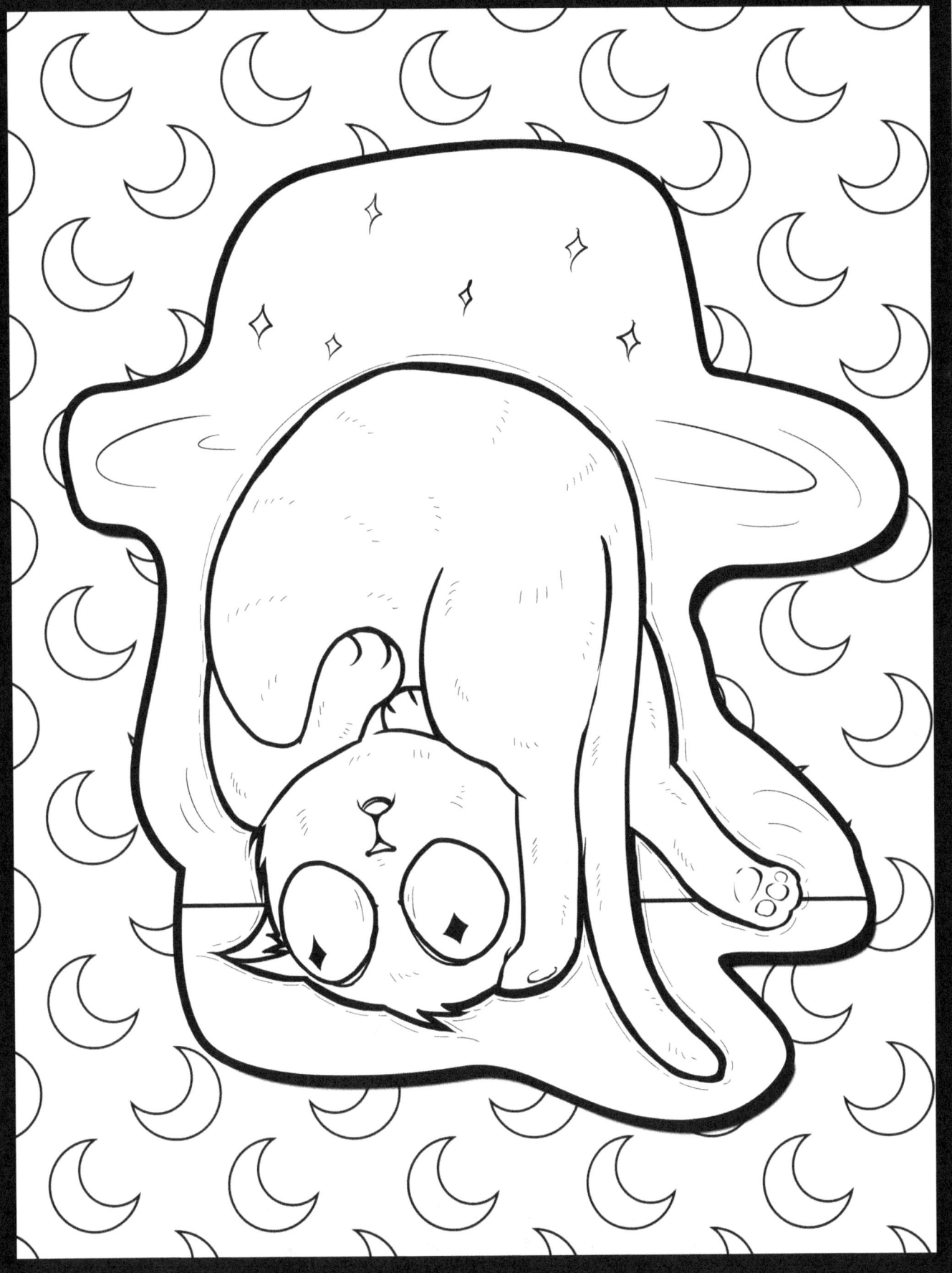

CAT BURGER

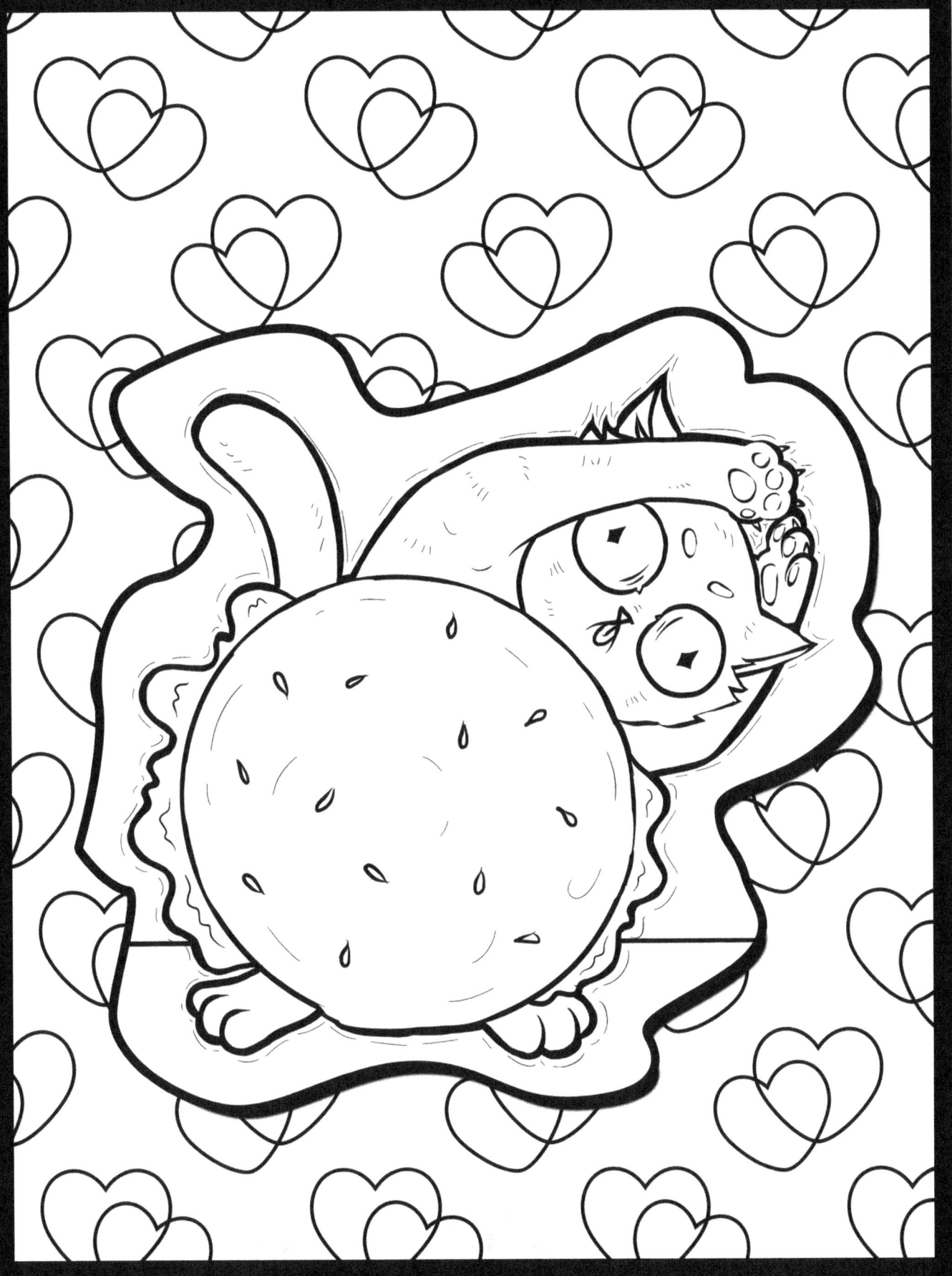

PAWDON ME!?

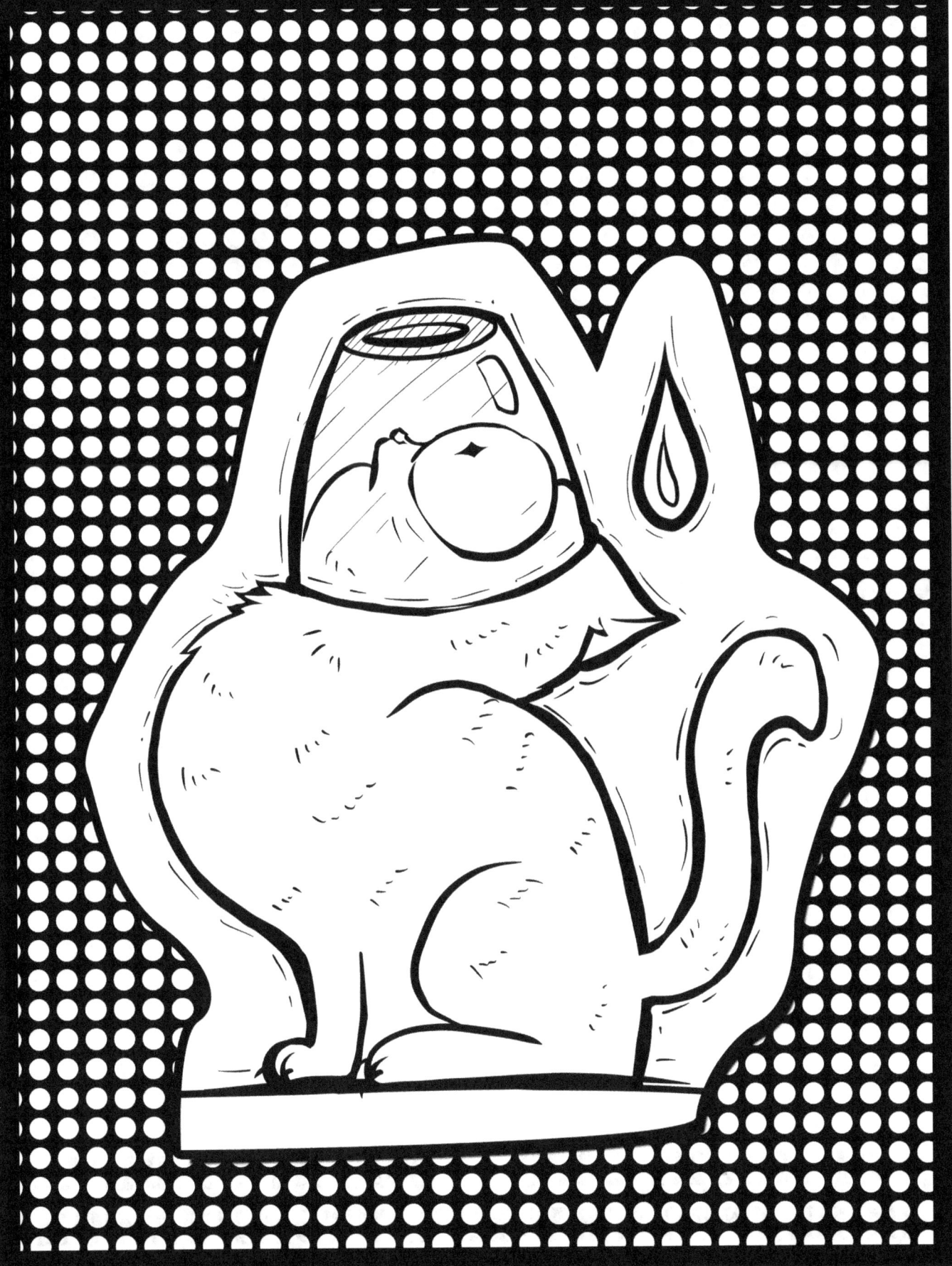

COPYRIGHT 2020 (THE ART OF BIDA)
MORE INFO WWW.THEARTOFBIDA.COM

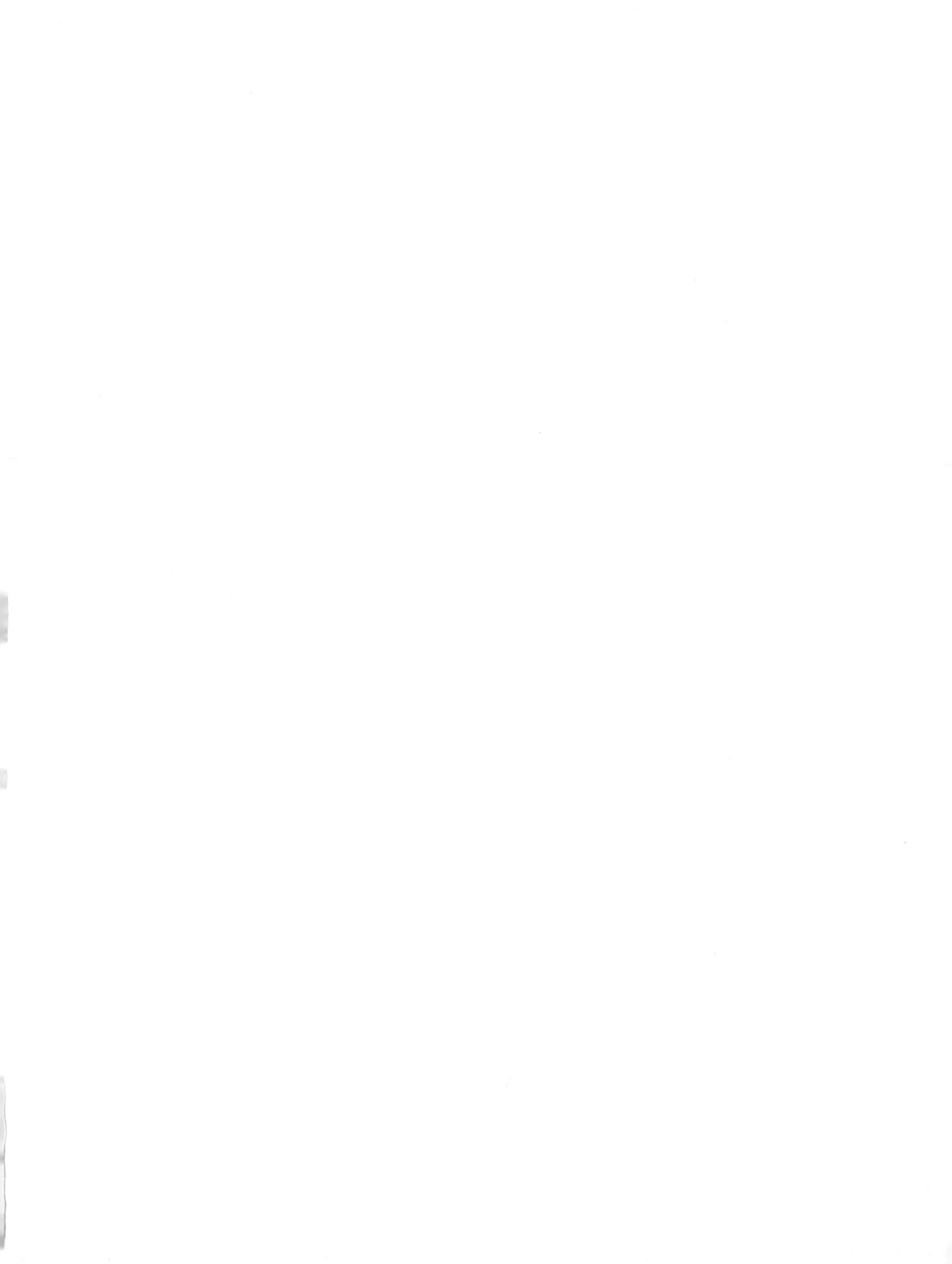

www.ingramcontent.com/pod-product-compliance
Lightning Source LLC
Chambersburg PA
CBHW080528220526
45465CB00006B/2636